Connected, transparent and committed

Connected, Serving the *transparent and* Surinamese society *committed* for 150 years

PETER SANCHES (ED.)

LM PUBLISHERS

A decorated locomotive in the depot, possibly during the opening of the Lawa Railway Line in Paramaribo, 1905.
Photo: Eugene Klein. Collection Rijksmuseum Amsterdam NG-2009-141-4

150 years of DSB

6   **Foreword**

9   **The development of the Surinamese economy 1865–2015**
The transformation from a plantation to a mining economy
    Winston Ramautarsing

37   **Suriname after 1863**
Social changes in a colonial society
    Jerome Egger

65   **Mining in Suriname**
Its past, present and future
    Glenn Gemerts

89   **No time to lose**
The importance of education to Suriname's development
    Marie Levens

103   **Deeply rooted in society**
De Surinaamsche Bank and corporate social responsibility
    Chandra van Binnendijk

115   **255 years of paper money in Suriname**
Surinamese bank and currency notes from 1760 to 2014
    Theo van Elmpt

143   **The art collection of the De Surinaamsche Bank**
A collection to be proud of
    Marieke Visser

Foreword

Dear Reader

As the Chief Executive Officer of De Surinaamsche Bank N.V. (DSB) it is with great pleasure and enormous gratitude that I recommend you read this book.

On 19 November 1989, then director Joseph A. Brahim wrote the following in *Verbonden* ('Connected'), the commemorative book that would be published to mark the bank's 125th anniversary: *'After some consideration, it soon became apparent that producing a commemorative book about DSB on such short notice would be unfeasible, since time was not on our side. The research that is required for such a commemorative book would mainly have to be conducted in archives in the Netherlands. We share this information with future bank directors, so that they can take this into account if they decide to compile a commemorative book to celebrate DSB's 150 year anniversary.'*

Now, 25 years later, we offer you a book that we believe would more than satisfy the former bank directors' wishes. A book that sheds light on Surinamese society from different perspectives and in which DSB – as part of this ever-changing society – has succeeded in building up and maintaining enough confidence to fulfil its role as a bank. The title of the book is therefore highly significant for us: *Connected, transparent and committed*.

We respect our past and are fully aware that DSB's relationship with the community is at the heart of our continuing existence. This connection is reflected in the excellent relations between the bank as an employer and its staff and their families, between the bank and its shareholders, and between the bank and the government.

Transparency is the guiding principle is our work

Increasingly, every banking institution must factor in laws and regulations in matters that are prescribed as mandatory; at DSB this is part of our corporate culture.

All our staff understand that as a bank, especially as the largest in Suriname, we bear a high degree of social responsibility and are therefore willing and able to justify our actions and transactions at all times.

'DSB is all about being involved'

I make this statement with pride, because for 150 years already we have adapted to changing circumstances with discretion and compassion and thus continued to serve our community, always upholding principles of ethics and respect. De Surinaamsche Bank cannot be anything but engaged with Surinamese society – the name of the country is part of the bank's name; Suriname in our genes.

Connected, transparent and committed contains contributions by several authors and would not have seen the light of day without the enthusiastic, determined, and most of all professional guidance provided by Ron Smit (publisher) and Peter Sanches (editor) of LM Publishers in the Netherlands. A great job well done!

I hereby thank the authors who accepted the commissions and who shed light on specific aspects of our history. And I ask you, the reader, to understand that each author has described his or her field of expertise from a particular perspective. We believe that allowing this intellectual freedom is vital to fostering transparent discussions about our past. That they will in turn inspire further interesting conversations is almost inevitable.

This book begins with an accessible overview of our economy by Winston Ramautarsing, who explains how it transformed from a plantation to a mining economy. The next chapter, by historian Jerry Egger, describes the changes that our society experienced during this transformation.

Glenn Gemerts shares his ideas relating to the ongoing discussions about the role and importance of the mineral sector to the ongoing development of our economy.

The chapter, 'No time to lose', by Marie Levens, emphasises the importance of education for our country's development – a subject very close to my heart. Our close involvement with Surinamese society compels us to consider this a call, even a cry of distress to policymakers to improve our education system as quickly as possible. We must equip our youth with knowledge and skills so that they can hopefully deal with the growing economic competition and continue to demand decent work. There is no (more) time to lose!

Chandra Binnendijk's chapter about corporate social responsibility and our bank speaks for itself. We will always position DSB as a citizen of this country and continue to support socially responsible activities without distinguishing between race, religion, political orientation and language.

Theo van Elmpt's contribution is very important; a good history of the development of Suriname's money is hard to come by and we are proud to share this description by an internationally renowned scholar. This chapter is quite detailed and covers a longer period than DSB has been in existence (1760 to 2014), but we think it enhances this book.

I found the contribution by Marieke Visser hard to place: is it 'journalistic artistry' or 'art-loving journalism'? I'm not sure. Marieke has done an excellent job in sharing our bank's art collection with you. Art and culture bring balance to our lives, alleviate the urge to consume and help us realise that everything exists in relation to everything else.

With the publication of *Connected, transparent and committed*, we especially want to express our gratitude to the people of Suriname. This book is a tribute to you all. We, De Surinaamsche Bank, are honoured to be part of this wonderful community. We are here for you and you can count on us; also for the next 150 years!

Happy reading.

Yours sincerely,

Sigmund L. J. Proeve

The development of the Surinamese economy 1865–2015

The transformation from a plantation to a mining economy

Winston Ramautarsing

The Republic of Suriname proudly became an independent nation in 1975. The history behind this transformation, however, goes back several centuries. The British founded Suriname as a colony in 1651 and began constructing sugar plantations along the Suriname River. During one of the many wars between the Netherlands and Great Britain, the Zeelanders conquered Suriname in 1667. When the Treaty of Breda was signed later that year, the colony remained in Dutch hands, having been exchanged for New Amsterdam, now New York City. In 1682, Zeeland sold its rights to Suriname to the West Indian Company (WIC), which in its turn sold them to the Chartered Company of Suriname, leaving the country in the joint possession of the WIC, the City of Amsterdam, and the Van Aerssen van Sommelsdijck family. After the dissolution of the WIC in 1792, the Dutch government took over the administration of the colony.

When Suriname came under Zeelandic rule in 1667, there were 170 plantations, which, through land reclamation, had expanded to 600 by 1770. A plantation in Suriname differed from a European farm in multifarious ways. Usually they cultivated only one product such as sugarcane or cotton, with the sole purpose of making a profit on the invested capital. To increase that profit as much as possible – which did not always happen – the plantation system was based on the immoral system of slavery and the trafficking and trade of humans.

On a financial-economic level, the plantation economy's peak had passed after the 1770s. After that, the plantations started to decline for several reasons. Many plantations were sold to investors who did not live in Suriname, or did not manage the plantations themselves, but left them in the hands of their managers, whose only task was to guarantee short-term results. Easy credit led to a series of bankruptcies, many Dutch plantation owners saw their money go up in smoke, and many plantations

Javanese vegetable hawker in Paramaribo, 1949. Collection Nationaal Museum van Wereldculturen, TM60057033

The Governor's residence on Waterkant in Paramaribo, printmaker Jacob Eduard van Heemskerck van Beest, Esq., Steendrukkerij de Industrie, Frans Buffa and Zonen, 1860. After a drawing by Gerard Voorduin. Collection Rijksmuseum Amsterdam, NG-1064

changed hands. A large group of concerned parties – bankers, mercantile houses, transporters and manufacturers – would still make handsome profits from the Surinamese plantations for many years. However, the second half of the 19th century saw the onset of the slow transformation of the Surinamese plantation economy into one based on mining. This chapter discusses that transformation.

The development and decline of the plantation economy 1863–1954

From a technical standpoint, the plantation system was a success. The production in the colony of tropical crops such as sugar, coffee, cotton, and cocoa increased spectacularly in the 19th century, and the consumption of these products in Europe grew accordingly. A series of innovations made the production of sugar in particular more and more efficient. Planters experimented with the best species and cultivation systems for sugar and coffee, and innovations spread fast. Most of the improvements were realised in the industrialised processing of sugar, and in the final refining in Europe. A thriving industrial sector came into existence in Amsterdam, where they processed the sugar from Suriname as well as that from other colonies.

Money in circulation

Parrot coin. Collection Central Bank of Suriname

The first coin in the Suriname colony was the 'Parrot coin' (*Papegaaienmunt*), introduced in 1679. It bore a depiction of parrot sitting on a branch with one, two, or four leaves. One leaf represented a pound of sugar, which cost 5 cents at the time. Because the coins cost a lot to make, it was decided in 1757 to use playing cards as Suriname's official currency. The cards had a nominal value, a stamp, and the signature of an authorised civil servant. Dutch money, which was imported, was used as legal currency as well, but transporting it on ships was risky and expensive. This is why in 1829 the Private West India Bank (PWIB) was founded in Paramaribo, which was authorised to issue a limited number of banknotes. When this bank ceased operating in 1848, banknotes were still in circulation, yet there was no place to store them centrally and circulate them again. This problem was solved by the foundation of De Surinaamsche Bank (DSB).

The Surinamese polder system proved to be very innovative for the time, too. One of the short sides of the oblong polder plantations flanked the river, where a network of dykes and sluices was used to control water flowing in and out of the fields. Because the rivers are tidal, the only force needed to drive this system came from the Atlantic Ocean. When the tide rose and the sluices were opened, water poured in through a canal system that extended deep into the plantation. When the tide was low, the water level in the river was much lower, too, so when the sluices were opened again, water streamed back along the sluices and canals to the river. This system was ideal for irrigation and drainage. Moreover, the canals served as efficient waterways to transport crops to the river, and from there to Paramaribo, and eventually by sea to Europe.

According to DSB's annual reports, there were frequent problems that negatively impacted on the plantation economy. These varied from persistent droughts to fluctuating sugar prices (partly because of the rise of beet sugar) and a shortage of manpower. After the Apprenticeship-system period, the lack of workers forced some plantations to switch from labour-intensive sugarcane cultivation to less labour-

View of a coffee plantation in Suriname. At right a dike with a water wheel. At left a boat on a canal. According to the signature made by Willem de Klerk after a drawing by A.L. Broekmann. Collection Rijksmuseum Amsterdam, SK-A-4087

intensive cocoa production. The opening of the Suez Canal in 1869 would undermine in particular Suriname's competitive position on Europe's sugar markets.

The lack of labour

Even before the abolition of slavery, plantations attempted to cope with the shortage of manpower by trying to attract immigrants to Suriname. The first group consisted of Dutch farmers, who settled in Upper Saramacca in 1845. This initiative failed, mostly due to poor preparation, and half the colonists died. Most of their descendants stayed in Suriname, and to this day these *'boeroes'* (*'boer'* is the Dutch word for 'farmer') form a small but visible part of the nation. The arrival of Chinese immigrants in 1853 did not solve the labour shortage, either.

The abolition of slavery in 1863 was a tough blow for the plantations. The planters not only suffered from a lack of manpower, but some of them also lost all hope for the future. After abolition, the former slaves were still forced to work on the plantations

A group of indentured labourers from British India in the so-called coolie depot in Paramaribo, 1891. In the foreground an English policeman.
Photo: Hendrik Dooyer.
Collection Rijksmuseum Amsterdam,
NG-1994-65-4-11-1

for ten years, but after this transition period, many of them turned their backs on the plantations and concentrated on working in forestry, mining, and the services sector. Initially, Hindustani contract labourers replaced them: after 1873, the government brought 30,000 of these British Indians to Suriname to work on the plantations for five years. After their contracts ended, they could choose to return or to stay: 11,000 of them chose the former. After 1890, it became more interesting for them to stay, as the colonial government began encouraging ownership of small parcels of farmland to grow food.

Because of nationalist opposition in India to this kind of labour migration the importation of British Indians ended in 1916. However, even after 1890, and following rebellions on several plantations by Hindustani immigrants, measures had been taken to maintain the inflow of immigrants: this time with contract labourers from Java, in the Dutch East Indies. Over 33,000 Javanese came to Suriname until the Second World War. Initially, most of them returned after their contracts ended, but, like the Indian immigrants, about two thirds of the Javanese contract labourers eventually settled in Suriname permanently.

The importation of contract labourers helped to postpone the winding down of the traditional plantation agriculture, but it could not halt the inevitable. The supply of workers from Java had ceased by the end of the 1930s because of the decline of the plantations. The manpower shortage was partly overcome by merging plantations. The number of plantations decreased rapidly. While in 1863, there were 216, in 1913 there were 79, and in 1940, only ten were active. The contribution of agriculture to export revenue decreased accordingly: from 80 per cent in 1863 to 6 per cent in 1940.

De Surinaamsche Bank building on the Gravenstraat in Paramaribo, Suriname, ca. 1870. Photo: E.L. (Emile Lancaster) Cramer. Collection Nationaal Museum van Wereldculturen, TM 60005714

De Surinaamsche Bank

When De Surinaamsche Bank (DSB) began operating in 1865, only 216 plantations remained. Slavery had been officially abolished two years earlier, and the Apprenticeship period – a time of transition – had started, during which the recently freed slaves were forced to continue working on the plantations for another ten years. In those days, the bank played a crucial role in the colony's financial affairs. By Royal Decree, the colonial authorities granted DSB the task of acting as a circulation bank in the colony for 25 years.

De Surinaamsche Bank was formally established in 1864 in Amsterdam, and started operating in Suriname in 1865. Despite the name, the company was registered in the Netherlands, and the share capital was mainly in Dutch corporate and private hands. However, the banknotes the bank issued did have Surinamese symbols and landscapes. After the first period of 25 years had passed, the patent was extended again by Royal Decree with some modifications in 1890, and repeatedly thereafter until 1957.

Javanese contract labourers harvesting sugarcane. Collection Rijksmuseum Amsterdam, NG-1994-65-25-2

The decline of the plantation economy

Besides the plantations, there were very few economic opportunities in the second half of the 19th- and the first half of the 20th century. The gold mines provided work for some of the former slaves, while the expanding civil service also created jobs. But there was hardly any industrial development in Suriname. Some new economic activities were initiated alongside the traditional ones, but most of these disappeared after some time. For a long time, traditional agricultural products remained the most important exports: sugar and its by-products, cocoa, coffee, and timber. Around the time of abolition, cotton production was past its prime – the final tons of this plantation product were exported in 1879.

Sugar exports fluctuated dramatically throughout the years due to developments on the international sugar market. The peak production year was 1931, when a record 20,414 tons was exported. The sugar plantations suffered severely from the manpower shortage, especially during the First World War, and the situation deteriorated when the importation of migrant labourers from British India ended in 1916, after which the colony was fully dependent on labourers from the Dutch East Indies. This problem had to be solved to attract new capital to the colony. It was decided to import 10,000 labourers from Java each year, but these numbers were never achieved.

Molasses, a by-product of sugar, was partly exported, mainly to North America, or used locally in the production of rum. The volume of molasses production and exports naturally depended on the sugar crops. Rum exports reached their peak in 1915, with 1.5 million litres sold abroad. Molasses was also used to produce alcohol for methylated spirits, but that was only sold domestically.

At the time of the abolition of slavery, cocoa production was limited, but it gradually rose, to peak in 1895 with the export of 4456 tons, making cocoa the most important crop in the colony at the end of the 19th century. Yet production decreased dramatically in subsequent decades, partly due to agricultural problems, including Witches' Broom disease, and by 1930, cocoa exports were negligible.

Statistics relating to coffee, one of Suriname's first export products, are even more irregular. There was a peak in 1935 with 4479 tons exported, but here, too, we see a gradual fallback to minimum levels. Aware of the difficulties experienced by the plantations, in 1935 the Dutch government extended 175,000 guilders worth of aid

The interior of the sugar factory on the Rust en Werk Plantation, four men standing by the boilers. Photo: Hendrik Dooyer. Collection Rijksmuseum Amsterdam, NG-1994-65-2-36-1

to the coffee farmers to restructure their companies. This amounted to 3.5 cents per kilogram of coffee produced, and was raised to 5 cents if it was used to start farming a different crop (oranges, for example).

Finally, logging has been important throughout Suriname's history, but timber exports have always been low. Exports increased after the Second World War, reaching circa 50,000 cubic metres on a yearly basis in 1950.

New alternatives

Unlike large-scale (plantation) agriculture, small-scale agriculture developed in a positive way, particularly rice cultivation. Around 1900 the country was almost completely dependent on imports to satisfy the demand for rice, but twenty years later its annual crop amounted to around 10,000 tons, enough for the entire colony. This growth was particularly stimulated during the First World War, when the colonial authorities started promoting the production of food crops. Some small farmers in Nickerie founded a rice husking cooperation, and some plantations even began farming rice. From 1922 production had grown to such an extent that some of the crop could even be exported.

Production of another product grew significantly in a brief period although its heyday was short-lived: latex, tapped from the balata tree. Extraction of balata sap (from which non-

Man with waste from the rice harvest.
Photo: Paul Romijn. Collection Nationaal Museum van Wereldculturen, TM 20033707

Reaping the rice crop with a combine harvester. Photo: Paul Romijn. Collection Nationaal Museum van Wereldculturen, TM 20033710

elastic rubber is produced) began around 1890 and peaked in 1913, when 1186 tons were exported, and about 2000 workers made a living from it. But around 1930, production costs – much like those of coffee and sugar – were higher than the market price. Cutbacks led to wide-ranging layoffs – this at a time when the unemployment rate was already rising because of Surinamese workers losing their jobs on Curacao and returning home. The government tried to stimulate citrus production, to no avail. Meanwhile, the demand for Surinamese balata decreased. Due to technological advances (such as the invention of synthetic rubber) and decreasing international demand, the sector could not compete, and around 1938, production came to an almost complete standstill.

Other alternatives to large-scale agriculture did not involve crops, but minerals: gold and bauxite. Even in the 16th- and 17th centuries, small groups of Europeans had looked for the El Dorado gold along the rivers of South America, sometimes successfully. However, gold production in Suriname officially started in 1876, and steadily grew, peaking in the periods 1892–94 and 1905–10, producing between 1000 and 1210 kilos a year. In the latter period, gold comprised 30 per cent of all export income, making it the most important sector in the economy. Around 4500 men worked in the gold industry. In 1900 the government constructed a railway line to facilitate access to the area, but shortly hereafter, the industry started to decline. After 1920, gold production sank to around 200 kilograms per year.

After a difficult beginning, bauxite production truly came online from 1922 in the area around Moengo. After 1936, and especially during the Second World War, bauxite was Suriname's main export. Bauxite ore is first processed into alumina, which is then melted to separate the aluminium metal. The Americans used Surinamese bauxite to manufacture fighter planes, which is why American troops were based in Suriname at the time. In 1946, Suriname was good for 60 per cent of the world's bauxite production, but this share rapidly decreased in subsequent years. In 1957, Suriname and the American corporation Alcoa signed the Brokopondo Agreement for the construction of an alumina factory, an aluminium smelter, and a hydroelectric power plant that would provide the energy for them. This project would be finished in the first half of the 1960s.

Government and population

To run their Suriname colony the Netherlands appointed a governor whose primary task was implementing decisions taken in the motherland. The upper echelon of society consisted of white plantation owners and Dutch civil servants. The social balance of power was reflected in the colonial Estates of Suriname, which was established in 1866. Of the thirteen members of the Estates, the governor appointed four and the others were elected through census suffrage, which entitled only people who paid the minimum amount of tax to vote. Consequently, less than 2 per cent of the people in Suriname could vote at the time.

The population's natural growth at the start of the 20th century was negligible, with a mortality rate of 2.2 per cent and a birth rate of 3 per cent. This can be put into perspective by comparing these statistics to neighbouring Guiana, which had the same birth rate, but a considerably higher death rate. Over time, the mortality rate decreased substantially to 1.4 per cent in 1930. While in 1920 the population counted 107,732, in 1930 it had grown to 133,650, a net growth of 23 per cent. This census did not include the 17,242 Maroons and 2404 indigenous people; at the time, they were still registered separately.

A country's economic development is inextricably linked to the education level of its people. When slavery was abolished, the level of education in Suriname was very low. Most of the few schools that existed were in Paramaribo, and they were in private hands. For instance, in 1844 the Evangelist Brotherhood started teaching the children of slaves and teachers in several districts, and the Roman Catholic Mission founded schools as well. The first public district school started accepting the children of freed slaves in 1867, and later also contract labourers' children. The Department of Education was founded in 1876, and a new education system was introduced, with compulsory education for all youngsters between 7 and 12 years old. Further advances happened slowly, however. When the Second World War broke out, there were only four advanced elementary and four advanced primary schools, all of them located in Paramaribo.

The effects of the Great Depression in the 1930s spurred the government's desire to be actively involved in the country's financial policy and it also wanted to determine the policy of De Surinaamsche Bank. At the time, many countries decoupled their

A Desa school in Santieholo. Children of Javanese migrants were taught some basic subjects in their own language here. They were deliberately excluded from the regular school system in an attempt to keep them on the plantations. Collection Nationaal Museum van Wereldculturen, TM 10019124

currencies from gold, which forced governments to tighten their grip, and Suriname was no exception. Until 1940, the Surinamese financial system ran in parallel to the Dutch one. In that year, the Surinamese guilder was uncoupled from the Dutch guilder and linked to the American dollar. Moreover, apart from De Surinaamsche Bank, which acted as an issuing and commercial bank, other banks were founded in the first half of the 20th century as well: the Surinamese Post Office Savings Bank (1903), Vervuurtsbank (1936, later changed to Hakrinbank), and the Municipal Credit Bank Suriname (1949).

A systematic start to diversification 1954–75

After the end of the Second World War, Suriname was granted a certain degree of autonomy, and in 1948, universal suffrage was introduced, so that in 1949 the entire adult population elected the Estates of Suriname. The Interim Regulation of 1950 and the Charter for the Kingdom of the Netherlands ('*het Statuut*') of 1954 defined the positions of Suriname and the Dutch Antilles. Suriname now had a say in its own internal affairs, which also meant that ministers were accountable to the Estates of Suriname.

The Charter redefined several of the responsibilities of Suriname's local government, for example, with regards to the monetary system. Suriname wanted to have more control over spending, monitoring, and underwriting the money in circulation, so the government decided to establish a central bank that was independent of the commercial banks. In 1950, they set up a banking commission, which had to define general financial policy, and the administration of DSB's commercial and issuing departments were separated. It was agreed to move the management of its issuing department from Amsterdam to Suriname, and new agreements were made regarding profit sharing and advancing financing of the country. On the basis of the Banking Law of 1956, the Central Bank of Suriname was founded in 1957 and assumed the responsibilities of an issuing bank. Its main function was to uphold the stability of the Surinamese guilder.

A new policy was devised to boost economic growth: systematic development. This meant that the Dutch government would direct the economic activities to a large extent. While during the Second World War bauxite had been an important source of income, after that the income from this sector had been low in terms of its contribution to gross domestic product and employment. The plantation economy had become very shaky, and many plantations ceased operating altogether. Moreover, the up-and-coming small-scale agriculture sector was characterised by low wages, poor infrastructure and water management, poor financing and unpromising markets, and insufficient knowledge of agricultural techniques among farmers. A Planning Office was set up in 1951 to improve conditions through systematic development, under supervision of the Netherlands.

Welfare Fund 1948–54

Because of the steady decrease in the amount of Dutch-owned plantations and the ensuing unemployment, the systematic approach was first and foremost aimed at the agricultural sector. Small-scale farming had to be professionalised and new polders constructed. To this end, the Welfare Fund was established, with reserves of 40 million Dutch guilders. The Fund financed the improvement of the Saramacca Polder drainage system and the construction of ten model polders such as the Nani Polder, the Groot-Henar Polder, the Prince Bernhard Polder, and the Wageningen rice polder. Other agricultural projects included stimulating rice farming in Coronie and reorganising coconut cultivation in the same district; the foundation of small businesses in Lelydorp; the foundation of a citrus export organisation and fruit processing company; the continuation of experiments with cocoa; the foundation of a cocoa propagation company; and steps to enhance the promotion of animal husbandry and fishing.

The construction of Wageningen rice polder and the creation of the Foundation for Mechanised Agriculture (SML) gave an extra impulse to small-scale farmers in Nickerie. In the so-called Middenstandspolder, in the shadow of Wageningen, 42 farms of 24 hectares each were set up. Moreover, the improvements to the polders made it possible to grow two crops per year instead of one. Furthermore, small business start-ups were stimulated.

The combination of a scale unprecedented in Suriname (around 10,000 hectares) and the introduction of new technologies was a significant leap forward, both quantitatively and qualitatively. The Nickerie farmers were very successful in applying the new techniques, which also resulted in the establishment of several large rice production and processing companies in the area. Unfortunately, several attempts to emulate this success in the districts of Coronie, Saramacca, and Commewijne yielded few results.

Apart from these agricultural projects, the Welfare Fund was used for several studies aimed at improving the implementation of the systematic approach: aerial surveys to assess natural resources, a new census, forest inventories, and a study of the country's hydropower potential. There were projects in the areas of public health and public housing (Beekhuizen, Zorg en Hoop). Funds were also spent on drawing up a 'comprehensive development and funding plan for Suriname', the basis for the Ten-Year Plan.

Under the Welfare Fund, developments in the colony were largely determined by events and decisions in the Netherlands. For instance, when the Dutch guilder was devalued in 1949, the value of the 40 million guilders in the Fund diminished by 20 per cent, and as a consequence several projects had to be cancelled. Furthermore, even though a large proportion of the Welfare Fund was used for agricultural projects, there was no integrated approach for this sector. For example, no attention was paid to factors like potential markets, cost prices, productivity, and freight tariffs. Yet this

Factory of the Foundation for Mechanised Agriculture (SML) in Wageningen in the Nickerie district.
Photo: Paul Romijn. Collection Nationaal Museum van Wereldculturen, TM 20033618

period did see the laying of the foundations for further systematic development under the so-called Ten-Year Plan.

The Ten-Year Plan 1955–67

The Ten-Year Plan, which was ratified into law in 1954, was intended to foster greater economic independence, and serve as a basis for further development and improved social services. Suriname would cover one third of the costs, the Netherlands would advance a third, and donate another third. Suriname's budget could not actually cover its commitment, partly because the operational costs of the committed investments had to be paid from the same resources. After 1963, Suriname's share was therefore supplemented with money from the European Development Fund (EDF). That same year the original Ten-Year Plan was extended by another two years, and the estimated funding was increased from 127 million guilders to over 207 million.

The economy developed dynamically during the planning period. New export commodities such as shrimp and fish were produced, as were import-replacing products like butter, margarine, cooking oil, soft drinks, cigarettes, cement, plastics, nails, milk, rum, beer and chipboard. Private investment was high during this period, employment increased, and unemployment fell back to 5 per cent. The growth of

The yard at the Bruynzeel Suriname Timber Company, which manufactured chipboard, plywood and other products. Photo: Roy Tjin

the small industry sector was remarkable, particularly as it did not receive targeted attention from the government, and was only allocated a small portion of the development aid.

In 1960, construction began on the Afobaka Dam, part of the Brokopondo project that was to provide the power for Alcoa's bauxite industrial complex. This was mainly funded with international private capital, as the Netherlands refused to participate. After the dam was finished in 1964, the reservoir started filling up. Because around 1400 square kilometres of their territory was flooded, more than 5000 Maroons were forced to leave their villages and move to new 'transmigration villages'. Economically speaking, the project was very successful. Suriname benefitted from the increased employment, and also from the rise in government income, because the export price of alumina and aluminium was much higher than that of bauxite ore. But there were downsides, too. The high wages in the bauxite industry affected the rest of the economy, which was less profitable and could not uphold the burden.

The economy flourished in the decade between 1957 and 1967, with an average annual growth rate of no less than 8 per cent, and a low average inflation of 3 per cent. This was a direct outcome of the Brokopondo project – a total investment of circa 300 million guilders. Furthermore, the activities resulting from the Ten-Year Plan and the Additional Construction Plan, with a total investment of 200 million guilders, had a significant effect on growth as well. Investments under the Ten-Year Plan were mostly in infrastructure.

Besides bauxite, the government had also been investing in the forestry sector since 1954, particularly in roads to improve accessibility to the forests, in rejuvenating the forests, and in researching and teaching about wood types that at the time were not considered commercially viable. Timber merchants also invested heavily in equipment, such as trailers and skidders (heavy vehicles used to drag cut trees out of the forests). The Bruynzeel Suriname Timber Company played an important role in the development of forestry and wood processing. The company was founded at the end of the 1940s, and mainly produced plywood and sawn and sanded wood. Until 1964, timber was Suriname's second export product, after bauxite. That year, timber exports accounted for 9 per cent of the country's total exports. Due to the strong growth of the bauxite industry during the years that followed, and the rise of rice, shrimp, and cooking bananas as export products, the share from wood exports declined to 3 per cent in 1975.

The first and second Five-Year Plan 1967–76

At the end of the Ten-Year Plan period, the Planning Office published a National Development Plan for Suriname for the following decade, which was ratified by the Council of Ministers at the end of 1965. Partly because the Netherlands no longer wanted to commit itself to another ten years, a selection was made from the list of projects for inclusion in the first Five-Year Plan. This covered the period 1967 to 1971, and the costs were estimated at 125 million guilders.

The emphasis now clearly shifted to the mining industry, which received almost a quarter of the funds for, among others, mapping and surveying (14.6 million), the Geological Mining Engineering Department (10 million), and preparing the West Suriname Project (5 million), where the government was setting up another bauxite centre. The agricultural sector received 22.5 million (for the construction of polders, the Victoria palm oil project, and the expansion of the banana growing area), forestry received 17 million (mainly for forest rejuvenation and the construction of forest infrastructure), and the industrial sector 2 million (for the creation of the National Development Bank). The first Five-Year Plan set aside 19 million guilders for infrastructure, half of which was meant for the East–West connection road. The social sector got a raw deal though, with around 8 million designated to public housing (Tammenga), healthcare, and education. This was significantly less than the 12 million guilders spent on general administration costs.

The first Five-Year Plan was financed by the Netherlands, half as a donation, the other half as a (mostly soft) loan. Once again, Suriname could apply to the European Development Fund (EDF). The EDF provided a total of almost 40 million guilders to fund several projects in agriculture (4 million), infrastructure (11 million for the New Harbour and 2.5 million for the Central Market, among others), and to build some schools (6 million).

The second Five-Year Plan (1972–77) was budgeted at 220 million guilders. Because Suriname became independent in 1975, the period was shortened halfway through. Pending projects and the remaining funds were transferred to the Multi-Annual Development Plan. At this point, 150 million guilders from the second Five-Year Plan had already been used in forestry and the mining industry (34 million), agriculture (20 million), infrastructure (31 million), social projects (17 million), for the preparation of

Bananas arriving on the conveyer line in the processing hall at Surland Banana Plantation. Photo: Paul Romijn. Collection Nationaal Museum van Wereldculturen, TM E12-20033895

Bunch of bananas on the Surland Banana Plantation at Uitkijk. Photo: Paul Romijn. Collection Nationaal Museum van Wereldculturen, TM 20033891

the West Suriname Project (12 million), and general management/administration (12 million). Funding from the Netherlands in this period was divided into a donation of 60 per cent, and a loan of 40 per cent. In 1972, the Surinamese government and the Dutch Agricultural Cooperative Bank established the Agricultural Bank as a joint venture. After independence, Suriname took over the latter's shares.

Looking back, the years 1968 to 1975 saw stagnation in growth, while towards the end of this period inflation increased significantly as a result of the international oil crisis. After the Brokopondo project was completed, private investments decreased; uncertainty about the country's independence contributed to this. Development aid enabled the government to keep the economy plodding along, but the climate for private investment deteriorated, employment in the market sector stagnated, and migration to the Netherlands increased.

Agriculture and animal husbandry

Of the 24 plantations in 1954, only Mariënburg Sugar Company remained in 1975. However, other forms of large-scale agriculture were initiated, which received around 15 per cent of the development aid. Small-scale agriculture was the main source of employment in this period. But while the population almost doubled, the number of small farmers decreased slightly. They were even outnumbered by the people working for the government: the percentage of the working population in civil service increased from 18 per cent in 1960 to circa 30 per cent in 1975.

The downward trend that had started all across the board in the cultivation of cocoa, coffee, coconuts, and corn continued. Only coconut production managed to survive for a while, but it waned too. The cultivation of sugarcane and citrus recovered somewhat in 1969, but after that the decline continued, in spite of the arrival of Haitian and

Station Belwaarde on the Suriname River, seen from the Marienburg Sugar Factory. Photo: Paul Romijn. Collection Nationaal Museum van Wereldculturen, TM 20033790

Guyanese cane cutters. The cultivation of sugarcane, once the most important crop, was abandoned completely in the late 1980s.

The timber sector was particularly important for local construction in Suriname, whereas the volume of wood exports remained limited. In this period, large-scale production for export was considered, and about 9 per cent of the development aid was spent on surveying and rejuvenating the forests, with wood pulp for paper foremost in mind. Around independence, timber exports remained level at around 50,000 cubic metres per year, which was but a fraction of the potential volume.

The agrarian sector also suffered the consequences of the mining industry's growth. Already in 1957, the president of Suriname's Central Bank stated in his annual report that it would negatively affect the cost and pricing structure of agricultural products. However, the increased attention for the agricultural industry meant that the plantation sector could be dismantled, and in addition to this, small-scale agriculture yielded good results as well.

Population and education

Suriname's population almost doubled between 1954 and 1975. Nevertheless, the government managed to provide most children with a basic education, with the exception of those living inland. The capacity of the secondary school system increased as well. However, the curriculum was not tailored to the needs of the economy: only 8 per cent of all students were professionals, and the planned expansion of the technical colleges, funded with development aid, was only partly achieved.

In 1968, the University of Suriname was founded by merging two institutes: the Law School, which taught lawyers, notaries and higher civil servants; and the Medical School, which trained physicians. Currently, the university has three faculties: social science, medical, and technological.

Transformation and diversification of the mining economy, 1975–2014

While it was something to be expected in a time of worldwide decolonisation and independence struggles, Suriname's announcement of its independence came as something of a shock. When in 1973 the newly elected Arron government announced that Suriname would be independent in two years, it sparked tensions across the country. The opposition refused to go along with it because of the lack of guarantees. The political tension translated into ethnic tension, and an unprecedented exodus ensued despite the prevailing favourable economic climate. In the period preceding and immediately after independence (1972–78), Suriname had a negative migration rate of 110,325 people, almost a quarter of the population at the time. The largest exodus occurred in 1974/75. Fortunately, partly thanks to pressure from the Dutch government, the most influential political leaders came to an agreement, after which Suriname could become a truly independent nation.

At that point, the country was characterised by a small, fragmented population with a relatively brief shared history, living in a young democracy. It had comparatively rich natural resources (fishing waters, forests, agricultural land, irrigation water, minerals), but only a limited domestic market and a poorly developed entrepreneurial class. With a quarter of the population overseas, the country was heavily orientated towards the Netherlands, which had promised 3.5 billion Dutch guilders in development aid; moreover, Suriname had a cumbersome and ineffective government.

The young republic started out debt free: the Netherlands had forgiven Suriname the 300 million Surinamese guilders the colony owed the motherland. However, paradoxically enough, Suriname's independence did not mean the two countries parted ways. Quite the contrary: they agreed that the Netherlands would guide Suriname to economic independence over a period of ten to fifteen years. Eventually, 35 turbulent years passed before the umbilical cord was cut. The development agreement was put on hold thrice by the Netherlands, and it wasn't until 2010 that the financial aid was exhausted.

There was not only an enormous amount of development aid available in the early years of independence, but also a surplus from the bauxite sector. Moreover, in 1974 Suriname managed to introduce a new tax on bauxite production, based on a decision from the International Bauxite Association (IBA). Many economists at the time felt that poorer countries were unable to save enough, and that a lack of funds was the most significant bottleneck in economic development, a problem that could only be solved with development aid. Independent Suriname initially had at its disposal substantial sources of income, but they were only two: bauxite and development aid. In the years 1983 to 1987, both sources would dry up almost simultaneously. Moreover, a side-effect of the volume of Dutch aid and the period for which it had been granted (since the colonial era) was that it paralysed the government – the constantly expanding civil service was ever more inefficient, while the creation of conditions for growth in the private sector had always been of minor importance.

Suralco's alumina factory in Paranam.
Photo: Roy Tjin

The Multi-Annual Development Plan

Immediately after independence, a start was made on implementing the Multi-Annual Development Plan. The Planning Office had an important role in the process, but was not assertive enough. Because the plan was funded with Dutch development aid, the Netherlands' influence was still strong, and not all decisions were taken in Suriname, even at this point.

For decisions relating to spending, a joint Netherlands-Suriname Development Cooperation Committee (CONS) was created. It had three Surinamese and three Dutch members, and was a powerful body because development aid was such a major source of income for the Surinamese economy. Through the creation of several sub-committees, also staffed by Surinamese and Dutch experts, the CONS became involved in policy preparation too. So it did not act as a controlling body, but as the final authority – a sort of supra government. In addition, because of the Planning Office's

A Surinam Sky Farmers agriculture plane spraying pesticides and/or seeds. These aircraft are mainly used in rice and banana cultivation.
Photo: Paul Romijn. Collection Nationaal Museum van Wereldculturen, TM 20033507

ineffectiveness and the lack of qualified Surinamese staff, the systematic identification, formulation and execution of projects did not properly occur.

Nonetheless, an average of around 135 million guilders of development aid was spent each year between 1975 and 1980. Although these were substantial amounts, the planned level of investment could not be achieved because of the limited absorptive capacity. Moreover, erroneous reporting about the execution of approved projects led to irritating delays in payments, and the progress of those projects stagnated. Attempts by the Dutch government to become involved in Suriname's development policy appeared to have backfired.

The implementation of the Multi-Annual Development Plan led to substantial investments in the public sector, which caused a strong growth in gross domestic product. However, a large portion of the aid was not used for projects that would structurally raise the young republic's earning capacity. The surpluses from bauxite were spent consumptively through the regular budget, mostly on the ever-expanding civil service. Much of the government's money was invested in mega projects, such as the West Suriname Project, without prior research as to whether any cost-effective private investments would follow. An example of this was a railway line in West Suriname that was constructed without establishing who would use it in the short term, and under which conditions. This enormous influx of investment overheated the economy and labour costs rose, making profitable private company investments unfeasible.

25 February 1980

The military coup in 1980 did not only change the government, but the economy too, and in significant ways. At first, the Netherlands supported the mainly civilian Chin A Sen government. The new rulers introduced radical changes to socio-economic and financial policy. For instance, the West Suriname Project, which had been so omnipresent in the Multi-Annual Development Plan, was put on hold in favour of smaller-scale agricultural and industrial projects, which were mainly aimed at creating and preserving employment.

Because the results were disappointing – partly due to governmental inexperience – the population's initial support for the coup rapidly diminished. At the same time, revenues from the bauxite industry lessened substantially, while the government kept public investment at a high level. This led to a significant budget deficit, which was mainly defrayed by issuing more currency, causing rapid inflation. The population sank into poverty, and trade and industry came to a standstill.

> ... throw a chair at development aid:
> which holds us in consumption's grasp
> instead of spurring us to production...
> From: *Throw a Chair*, by Dobru, Surinamese poet/politician

In 1981, development aid reached its peak with an investment of 250 million Dutch guilders. But the relationship with the Netherlands deteriorated, and in 1982 the Dutch government put the aid – about 9 per cent of the GDP at the time – on hold. In this period, political opposition in Suriname increased as well, leading to the December Murders of 1982, which still cast a shadow over political and economic progress to this day. Around the same time, global alumina prices dropped. As a stopgap, the government used its gold and exchange reserves. This allowed for a high investment level until 1984, but would strongly weaken the economy later on. At that point, it became painfully obvious to what extent Suriname depended on Dutch development aid and the bauxite industry.

Instead of eliminating the government's enormous financial deficit by limiting expenses, the authorities implemented opaque measures in 1984, including applying several different exchange rates and limiting imports, which completely disrupted what economic stability there was. The government refused to take the necessary measures, and instead of lowering consumptive expenditure, raised it even further. The next five years saw the budget deficit quadruple.

The Suriname Interior War (1986–92) worsened the situation even more, not only because of the direct costs of war, but also due to the enormous damage resulting from the destruction of means of production and the decline in growth in certain sectors. Timber exports came to a complete halt between 1988 and 1995, causing huge losses for timber merchants; fortunately, this sector recovered afterwards. After much international pressure, the Venetiaan administration's plans to allocate large concessions of a million hectares each to three Asian timber merchants were not implemented. After that, it would be mostly foreign companies with smaller concessions that restored production to a level above the 300,000 cubic metres achieved in 2013.

Re-democratisation

Forced by growing discontent with the military dictatorship and the economic and political situation in general, a re-democratisation process began in 1987. The opposition, united in the Front for Democracy and Development, won the elections by a landslide. At first, the Shankar government, installed in 1988, benefitted from the rising alumina prices and the resumption of Dutch development aid. However, it did not tackle the many obstacles encumbering the economy fast enough. Despite a large majority in the National Assembly, this government lacked the decisiveness necessary in this post-military period, leaving an opening for the army to seize control once more, in the so-called telephone coup of 24 December 1990.

Organising new elections was the main task of the Kraag/Wijdenbosch administration, which governed for the following eight months, yet it could not dispel people's aversion to the military authorities, despite its populist approach. The first Venetiaan administration came to power with a vast majority in the 1991 elections, the year that also marked the low point of the crisis. Excessive budget deficits had exhausted the country's foreign currency reserves, and there were parallel foreign currency markets, upward spiralling inflation, and capital flight. The budget deficit tripled in a year, inflation was extremely high, and economic activity in the formal sector decreased worryingly. Those circumstances compelled the government to take macro-economic measures, but it wouldn't be until 1995/96 that a semblance of monetary stability was achieved. After a 396 per cent peak in 1994, inflation shrank to zero in 1996, and the exchange rate of the Surinamese guilder to the American dollar stabilised. The inefficient implementation of the programme of adjustments and the sacrifices the population had to make led to a decrease in public support for the government, and as a consequence, the presiding coalition failed to win enough seats to retain power after the 1996 elections.

The new Wijdenbosch/Radhakishun government, dominated by prominent figures from the military period, was very ambitious and radically changed the country's course. History seemed to be repeating itself: Public spending was increased substantially, the budget deficit had tripled, and the economy was shrinking. Yet again, more currency was issued to address the deficit, once more leading to high inflation and an uncontrollable exchange rate. This caused a second large wave of impoverishment that aroused great discontent among the population, who expressed their frustration in street protests. The government was forced to call snap elections in May 2000, which it lost.

This time, the disruption was less severe, and the new Venetiaan administration was able to restore monetary stability relatively quickly. The Netherlands offered ample guarantees to support the Surinamese currency. This government once again was tasked with redressing the economic balance. The currency was devalued, several product subsidies were stopped, and water and electricity rates were increased, but because the global economy was experiencing an upturn, the economy could be stabilised in a socially less painful manner than before. The strong increase in gold and oil prices not only dramatically increased the inflow of foreign currency, but also income from taxation.

In this period, the Surinamese dollar (SRD) replaced the Surinamese guilder using a fixed conversion rate of 1:1000 (this was called 'scrapping the zeroes'). Because of the massive budget deficit and the excess of money circulated by the Central Bank of Suriname, the number of banknotes in use had grown to such an extent that this financial reconstruction was necessary. Moreover, the government wanted to prevent a repetition of previous abuses of public funds. For instance, a new law was enforced that set a maximum limit on direct credits from the Central Bank of Suriname to the State, with sanctions imposed on the Bank's president in the event of infringement.

Introduction of the Surinamese dollar (SRD). Private collection

The mining industry

Suriname's small open economy was, and still is, sensitive to external shocks and the whimsy of global markets. Between 1975 and 2014, such fluctuations had directly affected mineral extraction and export. The most striking development was the diversification of the mining industry: it was expanded with oil and gold.

The bauxite sector had its ups and downs during this period. The government had to intervene in the mid-1980s and rescue the sector by abolishing the bauxite tax. The industry recovered after this, but the global economic crisis that began in 2008 delivered a heavy blow. Billiton-Suriname left the country a year later; Suralco had to cut its production in half, but did continue to supply the power generated from the reservoir to Suriname's national electricity company, which is very lucrative. In spite of this, Suralco is considering resuming regular production in Suriname.

Started from scratch in 1980, the state oil company Staatsolie N.V. – State Oil – has become Suriname's largest commercial enterprise. With an annual production of around five million barrels, it had a turnover of over one billion US dollars in 2013. In 2014, the refining capacity was raised from 7000 to 15,000 barrels per day. Thanks to higher international oil prices, State Oil's taxes and dividends have become the State's largest source of income.

The small-scale gold mining industry was reinvigorated at the end of the 1980s. Maroons and between 10,000 and 20,000 Brazilian *garimpeiros* (small-scale gold miners) worked in this industry. After the government, the gold mining industry provides the highest number of jobs, of which only a few are in the formal sector. This form of mining is extraordinarily lucrative, but global markets are fickle, and the methods, particularly the small-scale ones, significantly damage the country's environment, and are regarded as endangering the population's health. Large-scale gold mining only really took off in 2004, with the Gross Rosebel mine, collectively

Large-scale gold mining by Iamgold.
Collection Iamgold

owned by South African company Iamgold (95 per cent) and the Surinamese State (5 per cent).

Agriculture and animal husbandry

The agrarian products that formerly dominated the Surinamese economy have disappeared or diminished dramatically. Because of the high profits from the mining industry, even crops that grow well only form a relatively small part of Suriname's production. The amount of cultivated ground has decreased in the past few years: from 35,000 hectares in 2001 to 31,681 hectares in 2012.

Rice cultivation grew dynamically again during the 1980s with 300,000 tons of paddy rice produced and 140,000 tons exported in 1986. This was largely thanks to favourable prices on the European market; moreover it ensured that ample investments were made in expanding the irrigated rice fields. When rice prices declined at the end of the 1980s, the areas under cultivation did too. Nowadays, around half of the polder area is being planted, the better part of which is in Nickerie; exports now amount to roughly 50,000 tons per year. Banana production was significantly boosted by the restart of the State-owned company Surland (achieved with substantial subsidies from the European Development Fund), and exports rose from 30,000 to circa 80,000 tons per year. However, as the company continued to make a loss in spite of this, it was sold to the French-owned UNIVEG Group in 2014.

Animal husbandry, which produces exclusively for the domestic market, showed modest growth across the board. Milk production diminished, but the quantity of beef, pork and chicken doubled. The fishery sector flourished in this period. Particularly the trawler fleet was dramatically expanded, partly as a consequence of the arrival of the American company, Bumble Bee Industries. A transformation occurred in this sector: due to diminishing catches of the large marine prawns, fishermen switched to the smaller Atlantic seabob prawns. Furthermore, annual fish catches increased dramatically and fish exports grew to over 15,000 tons on a yearly basis.

There had always been a modest shortfall between food imports and agricultural exports. However, from 1974, things turned around, mostly thanks to the strong rise in fish and shrimp exports. Because of the considerable increase in export revenues from the mining industry, food imports have grown substantially, yet despite the country's agrarian potential, recent years have seen food imports outweigh exports again.

Government and citizens

One of the positive changes the military regime set in motion was a greater focus on education and literacy, particularly for disadvantaged communities. In 1980, the illiteracy rate in Suriname was a disquieting 17 per cent among men of 15 years and older, and 25 per cent among women. The efforts that have been made since have reduced the illiteracy rate to less than 10 per cent of the total population in 2014.

Employment fluctuated in Suriname from 1975 to 2014 as well. Apart from State Oil, the government – in large part using Dutch development aid – created several other State-owned companies, such as Patamacca, the Foundation for Agricultural Development in Commewijne (SLOC), the Multi Purpose Corantijn Canal Project (MCP), the Centre for Fisheries Harbours Suriname (Cevihas), and Surinam Timber. Most of them disappeared again quietly, so the jobs these companies provided went up in smoke. Moreover, it became a political tradition for ruling parties to reward loyalists with government jobs, regardless of their skills or commitment. Including semi-governmental companies, the government grew from employing 30 per cent of Suriname's working population in 1975, to circa 60 per cent in 2014. Yet the effectiveness of the state apparatus seemed to diminish ever more noticeably.

With support from the Inter-American Development Bank and the United Nations Development Programme, specific policy proposals were formulated to downsize and streamline the civil service, decrease 'red tape', and increase productivity. But as with the intentions to privatise ailing State companies, successive governments, regardless of their political background, have done little to achieve these goals. What has been improved is the levying of taxes and their collection, the financial justification of the long-term budget, the financial planning, and inter-ministerial cooperation.

Introduction of the China UnionPay (CUP-card), a prepaid debit- and credit card by DSB in Suriname. Governor Gillmore Hoefdraad from the Central Bank of Suriname delivers a speech at the presentation of the new payment method. Collection DSB

The sitting government lost its majority in the 2010 elections, and the Bouterse/Ameerali government was formed. Since then, Suriname's economy has kept growing: GDP has increased by around 4 per cent. This growth is mainly due to investments in public infrastructure, the gold mining sector, and the oil industry, including the oil refinery. However, the excessive government spending since the second half of 2013 has led to a downswing in State finances, increasing public debt, and diminishing gold and foreign exchange reserves. International credit rating agencies Fitch, Moody's, and Standard and Poor's have indeed announced positive prospects, but warn that debilitation of budgetary discipline could easily result in erosion of the achieved stability. The roughly 25 per cent drop in the gold price once again underlines the dangers of a unidirectional development strategy in which the mining industry – centred on gold, bauxite and oil – dominates.

Challenges to an enduring economic future

In economic terms, over the past 150 years, Suriname has made an impressive leap forward from a plantation economy that was largely dependent on the capriciousness of nature, to a modern mining economy. Originally set up as the food barn of tropical produce for the motherland, the colony, influenced by international developments and local relations, gradually grew to become an independent nation. The direction of the economic and social dynamics was completely in the hands of the motherland at first, but it was increasingly *Surinamised*.

Material wealth has increased at an average of 2 per cent per year since 1954. This relatively low growth was partly due to the economic malaise in the decade between 1984 and 1994, which has only moderately increased to over 4 per cent from 2004 to 2013. The exodus at the time of the country's independence seriously dented Suriname's human potential, both quantitatively and qualitatively.

Besides the advances when it comes to infrastructure, health, education, and civic participation, Suriname also faces some challenges. Climate change – something a small country cannot do much about – is an important one. Adequate protection is therefore vital, especially of the coastal areas, where rising sea levels pose a tangible threat. But opportunities can be created too, for instance, making international agreements about, and benefitting from the conservation of the tropical forests.

Suriname is a country blessed by nature, yet a large part of our population lives in unacceptable social-economic conditions. Material prosperity and social security are at a lower level than they should be (considering the country's natural wealth), not enough employment is created, and wages are too low. Income distribution continues to widen, which can only lead to growing inequality and social tensions that could also inflame ethnic tensions. There is growth, but with a limited development that is not enduring.

The current relative prosperity is mainly attributable to the increased exploitation of the country's mineral resources. This increased wealth, however, is not sustainable: it is dependent on the vagaries of the global market, and moreover, natural resources are finite. A new policy should be formulated in the near future, one in which less of the proceeds from the mining industry are spent, and as much as possible is invested in buttressing the competitiveness of sustainable sectors, such as agriculture, animal husbandry, fishing, forestry, hydropower, and ecotourism. The ambition to become the region's food barn, which would require a massive increase in agricultural exports, cannot be a pipedream, as it is absolutely essential to creating lasting wealth in the long term. Sustainable economic growth in Suriname is only possible with a good macro- and micro-economic policy, based on national savings, and augmented by international loans of amounts the national economy can sustain.

Changes, however, do not come by themselves. The Surinamese people will have to select a new generation of leaders based on integrity, economic policy, and results. Under good leadership, Suriname can become a wealthy country. But to achieve this, we need to alter our fundamental approach. There is an urgent need for a widely supported programme of reforms targeting the public sector, paralleled by a concurrent programme stimulating national production and job creation in the private sector. This would form the basis of a modern, dynamic and durable economy for Suriname in the future.

Winston Ramautarsing (M.Sc.) studied development economics and has been a management consultant and managing director of PROPLAN Consultancy since 1992.

Literature

General Bureau of Statistics, *Balansen van de nationale economie en aanvullende staten. Suriname in cijfers.* General Bureau of Statistics, 1975.

Caram, A.R., *Ontsporingen op weg naar monetaire soliditeit: de drie fasen in het bestaan van de Centrale Bank van Suriname.* Paramaribo: Central Bank of Suriname, 2007.

Central Bank of Suriname, *Vijf en twintig jaren Centrale Bank Van Suriname 1957 April 1982*, Paramaribo: Central Bank of Suriname, 1982

Central Bank of Suriname, Annual Report 1965.

Central Bank of Suriname, Annual Report 1976–80.

Central Bank of Suriname, Annual Report 1982–85.

'De economische toestand van Suriname in 1935', in: *Jaarverslag van de Kamer van Koophandel en Fabrieken 1936.*

De Surinaamsche Bank N.V., Annual Reports from 1873 to 1952 (Amsterdam).

IMF, Article IV: Mission. IMF, 2013.

Loor, A.H., 'Suriname: een historiek', in: *Vlaanderer*, vol. 46 (1997).

Rooij, W. de & M. van Schaaijk, *Ekonomische ontwikkeling van Suriname: een inleiding.* Paramaribo: Vaco, 1983.

Schaaijk, M. van, 'Mamidat' (www.stuseco.org)

Sedney, J., *Het werkgelegenheidsaspect van het Surinaamse tienjarenplan.* Amsterdam: J.P. Bakker, 1955. (Dissertation)

Suriname after 1863

Social changes in a colonial society

Jerome Egger

When De Surinaamsche Bank was founded on 19 January 1865, it was a time of great economic, political, and socio-cultural changes for Suriname. Slavery had been abolished: on 1 July 1863, around 34,000 men, women and children were freed, and nearly 10 million guilders were paid in damages – to the masters, not the victims. Former slaves had to find their own way in the colonial society, which in its turn had to grow accustomed to the idea that there no longer were any people who could randomly be forced to do any kind of work. After all, in the eyes of the colonial rulers, the plantation economy was only viable if there was an unbroken supply of cheap labour. After abolition, new cultural groups were introduced to the colonial society, who had to try to assimilate into this piece of the Netherlands on the South American continent.

In 1865, Suriname established a colonial parliament, which was supposed to become the voice of the local population. The majority of that population, which had been enslaved for so long, now had to take matters into its own hands and map out a route for itself – in a society that was strongly oriented towards Europe, rather than the people's countries of origin. Attempts to assimilate the various groups, leading to a general acceptance of the Dutch cultural legacy among all Surinamese people, would be only partly successful.

Over the course of several decades, the colonial society changed – new economic sectors flourished, and the different cultures nuanced the dominant Western ideal. The colony decided to move forward on its own, and on 25 November 1975, Suriname became an independent state. In subsequent years, things didn't always go the way many people had hoped, but eventually, progress came in the 21st century. The economy underwent a period of prosperity, when the government made a considerable amount of money thanks to the profitable prices of important raw materials such as oil and gold on the global market. Furthermore, the better part of the population was no longer Dutch-born, but Surinamese. So, since 1863 Suriname has grown into a multi-ethnic and multicultural country, with a modern economy, a democratic parliamentary system and, culturally speaking, with room for different groups to create their own

Slaves working the land, ca. 1850.
Collection Rijksmuseum Amsterdam, NG-2013-22-19

Post Gelderland and Jodensavannah, after a drawing by Gerard Voorduin.
Collection Rijksmuseum Amsterdam, G1-NM-10646

institutions. This chapter discusses the socio-historical changes in Surinamese society that followed the abolition of slavery.

The Apprenticeship system 1863–73

The abolition of slavery in 1863 did not mean complete freedom for the former slaves, who from that moment were regarded as the Creole community, a term that had already been accepted for a long time. For ten years, the liberated labourers were forced to work on the plantations under State supervision, although now they were being paid. The Dutch adopted this approach from the British, who, after abolishing slavery in their colonies in 1834, had implemented a period of apprenticeship, during which the Creoles had to work on the plantations as well. After intense protests, this system was abolished too, as it was little more than a perpetuation of slavery. Because of this most history books about the Caribbean consider 1838 as the year slavery actually ended.

In Suriname, the Apprenticeship system was less rigid. In fact, planters often complained that they had little or no control over the labourers. Clearly there was a huge difference between what the colonial society expected of former slaves and how the slaves themselves wanted to shape their lives. This clash resulted in the stereotypes about the Creole's supposed tardiness about working – typecasting that exists to this day. This does not detract from the fact that these people have had to work extremely hard to survive and hold their own. Many of them continued working on the plantations, while others opted for small-scale agriculture: this enabled them to be self-sufficient, and to sell any surpluses at local markets.

Foreseeing the demand for land for small-scale agriculture, the colonial authorities had taken pre-emptive measures. Shortly before abolition, settlements were built for the former slaves, where they could obtain a plot of land for themselves and their families. At first, these settlements were located near the plantations, so that small-scale farmers could work there as well during harvesting time, when many labourers were needed. This is why the government deliberately did not assign large plots to anyone.

Immigration

The government stimulated immigration to expand the workforce. Dutch farmers and Chinese contract labourers were brought to Suriname even before the abolition of slavery, in 1845 and 1853, respectively. During the Apprenticeship system period, workers from different West-Indian areas, such as Barbados, Saint Lucia, and British Guyana, were brought to the colony as well. However, none of these measures supplied enough labourers for the plantations. A large number of the Dutch farmers died from illness and hardship after their arrival, and those who survived and stayed were independent men and women who grew crops and bred livestock on their own pieces of land. At the end of the 19th century, they became reasonable successful in the city and its surroundings. When their contracts ended, the Chinese changed professions: for instance, they began working as travelling salesmen, and later started their own small stores on the corners of the streets of Paramaribo, and in the districts. It did not work out for the West-Indian workers, either. They came to Suriname with high hopes for their new lives. But the abolition of slavery did not mean that the plantation owners' mentality had changed as well, leading to clashes between these labourers and the planters. By the end of the 19th century, the West-Indian workers and their children would increasingly find employment in the gold sector and the balata industry, where they could make a decent living.

Contrary to what the planters had feared, despite the lack of labourers the agricultural sector did not collapse at the end of the Apprenticeship system period. In the ten years after 1863, the Creoles had managed to advance their agricultural activities. For example, some had collectively bought plantations, with several families working the land. There were also places like Coronie, where, to the satisfaction of the colonial government, people grew food for their own families as well as for the market. And yet, the need for workers remained, especially for the plantations, which largely catered to the export market.

Socio-economic developments 1873–1900

An important event in the history of Suriname was the arrival of the first British-Indian (Hindustani) contract labourers, in 1873. The idea was that a steady supply of new workers from South Asia would not only ensure the survival of large-scale agriculture for the country, but that it could also be developed. According to the Colonial Reports, the government was happy with these immigrants. Their work ethos, frugal lifestyles, and longing to progress were seen as the positive influences the colony needed.

However, it soon became clear that even these people did not intend spending the rest of their lives on a plantation. When their contracts ended, many tried to buy a plot – building an independent life for themselves was their primary concern. This became easier after 1895, because from that year on, they were allowed to acquire land without losing the right to return to India. Some Hindustanis started cultivating rice – the wet variety – in Nickerie, among other places. But rice was not the only successful food crop. Small-scale farmers in the surroundings of Paramaribo became serious competitors to the Dutch farmers who produced vegetables, fruit, and milk for the city. The Hindustanis managed to conquer the better part of that market. Subsequently, many city residents who wanted fresh produce on their table every day became dependent on them.

Rice cultivation continued to increase – the land around Nickerie proved to be ideal. With enormous effort, the Hindustanis managed to produce more and more rice, eventually eliminating the need for imports of this staple food. Consequently, for some former contract labourers, rice cultivation became a stepping-stone from the simplicity

Hindustani indentured labourers in the coolie depot, 1891.
Collection Rijksmuseum Amsterdam, NG-1994-65-4-11-1

of small-scale agriculture to the middle class, with a more than decent income. The colonial government, recognising that this sector could increase agricultural production and cultivate a new export product, initiated an incentives policy, for example, by allocating land.

Gold and balata

Other economic activities began in the last quarter of the 19th century. When gold was found in neighbouring French Guyana, the government woke up. There was a good chance that the precious metal would be found in eastern Suriname as well, since the geology was very similar to that of the French colony. An increasing number of requests for gold prospecting permits were honoured, and they soon found the first gold. Interest in looking for the metal grew not only in Suriname, but in the Netherlands as well. Private enterprises and individual gold prospectors were granted concessions.

Washing the gold in the Placer de Jong gold mining area in Suriname.
Photo: Julius Muller. Collection Nationaal Museum van Wereldculturen, TM 60009011

Tapping balata. Collection Nationaal Museum van Wereldculturen, TM 10030621

However, all attempts at setting up large companies in the inhospitable area failed. The government tried to stimulate a large-scale gold industry by building a railway line to the east, but it was not profitable, and the costs of the project burdened the national budget for years afterwards. On the other hand, for people living along the railway line, the train was a godsend: now they could reach the city much faster to sell their products. Travelling by train in the opposite direction – from Paramaribo to the smaller cities in the country during holidays – was a real happening. But the actual goal of fostering the gold industry was not realised. Individual prospectors ('*porknokkers*') managed to keep going for some time, but when the gold-bearing ore that was closest to the surface had been stripped, their numbers shrank as well. It wasn't until the 21st century that it became clear that there are still large amounts of recoverable gold in the ground.

The balata industry was another important economic sector in Suriname. Balata, natural latex produced by balata trees, turned out to be very suitable to make non-elastic rubber. Rubber was used for tyres in the burgeoning car industry, and as isolation material for submarine cables. As demand grew, so did the balata industry. Balata trees could mostly be found in West Suriname. Large groups of workers remained in the interior of the country for months at a time, in order to tap as many trees as possible and collect the sap. They made a decent living, but, as is often the case, the buyers earned the most. The gold and balata industries were mainly dominated by the Creoles. This was no coincidence, seeing as the government had instated specific laws forbidding the Hindustanis from participating in the forest industries. The government insisted that they had been brought to Suriname to work on the plantations, not in other sectors of the Surinamese economy.

New agricultural sectors

Thanks to this diversification, the Surinamese economy became less dependent on the plantation economy, especially sugarcane production. Cocoa played an important role as well. This product had been cultivated in Suriname for ages, but high prices on the global market around 1900 stimulated the production. Cocoa trees were planted on the plantations, but several small- and medium-size farmers made money from them as well. The export of cocoa beans was also very profitable for the government: in 1900, profits were almost twice as high as those from gold or sugar exports. However, the cocoa bloom came to an end due to a plant disease. Witch's broom petrified the beans, making them useless. By the time the disease was under control, competition on the global market was soaring. Other countries could produce cocoa on a larger scale at more competitive prices.

Plant diseases also put an end to another promising crop: bananas. In the second half of the 19th century, Americans had spread their wings over the Caribbean and Central America. This resulted in large banana plantations in several countries, including Jamaica. Suriname was interested as well. Bananas had been known there for a long time already, and were part of the diet of several communities, but there was no wide-scale, commercial cultivation. The country started growing bananas, but the plants

were stricken with Panama disease, destroying the crop and immediately ending the short-lived experiment. It wasn't until the 1960s that Suriname was able to produce and export bananas again. It would become one of the country's export mainstays.

Social and cultural developments 1863–1900

After 1863, the Netherlands envisaged a Surinamese society along Western lines. This vision was embodied in an assimilation policy that was rooted in the idea that the colony had to be Western in order for it to progress. Compulsory education would help the population, the Dutch language became a priority, and Western cultural expressions would be the norm. But the reality in Suriname was different. The Maroon and indigenous peoples had their own traditions, languages and cultural expressions that were far removed from the Dutch ideas. In the city, the Creoles managed to preserve part of their culture, despite desperate attempts from both within and outside the community to set European standards. Asian contract labourers brought to Suriname did have limited opportunities to express their culture, despite the attempts of several Christian groups to have them join their churches.

Nevertheless, the assimilation policy did have an effect on the society. On the surface, a visitor to the country during the early 20th century could have had the impression of being in a remote province in the Netherlands. Education was taught in Dutch, so those who had attended school spoke the language. Newspapers were in Dutch too, as were the debates in the Colonial Council. Cultural life was dominated by Western plays, literary evenings and music performances. Important Christian institutions such as the Roman Catholic Church, the Evangelist Brotherhood, and the Lutheran and Reformed communities had a notable presence on the streets of Paramaribo.

Picking the fruit of the cacao tree, 1920. Photo: Augusta Curiel. Collection Nationaal Museum van Wereldculturen, TM 60005761

But below the surface, the story was quite different. The language on the streets was Sranan, and the various indentured labourers all spoke their own languages. This was partly due to the government's own policy: at the so-called *coolie schools*, British-Indian contract labourers were taught in their own language. Creoles had their own religion, *winti*. This was prohibited, as it was seen as idolatry, yet there were important locations in backyards, outside the city, and in the Para district where these religious beliefs were practised. At first, the contract labourers built small Hindu temples and mosques, which would later become visible places of worship. The various communities had their own popular plays, which were performed on special occasions. Often, music at parties, religious events and other occasions was not Western either. And Asian indentured labourers often wore their traditional clothing, at least until the mid-20th century, while Creole women walked around in *kotomisi* and *angisa*. Thus, enough of each culture survived to preserve a rich, multicultural society for later generations.

Suriname until the Second World War 1900–1940

Suriname changed on several levels during the first half of the 20th century. Bauxite made its entry into the country's economy and would dominate it. Non-Christian religions were institutionalised, the education system became more accessible to more people, and on a political level, the Colonial Council became the Estates of Suriname. Hindustani and Javanese men were admitted to this body – no longer was it the exclusive domain of the light-coloured Creole elite. Increasing numbers of Surinamese were leaving the country – some temporarily, others for good – to study or seek work elsewhere. Radio began forming a part of Surinamese life, as did foreign films, a relatively cheap form of mass entertainment that became hugely popular.

Kotomisi with *angisa*, ca. 1900.
Photo: Eugen Klein. Collection Rijksmuseum Amsterdam, NG-1994-32-13

Large-scale agriculture on the plantations declined considerably, economically speaking. For instance, the coffee trade flourished for a short time during the 1920s, with an enormous peak in 1925, but after that, sales and production decreased. Only a few plantations managed to operate satisfactorily for a while, such as Mariënburg, the modern sugar factory owned by the Nederlandse Handel Maatschappij (NHM). On the other hand, small-scale agriculture thrived. Small farmers were producing for their own use, the local market, and, on a limited scale, for exports. The colonial government contributed with land allocations, and by creating facilities for agricultural loan banks and credit corporations.

Forestry activities decreased. Large companies had turned their back on the gold industry. Balata enjoyed a last, brief period of prosperity in the 1920s, when it once again became an important export product, but in the 1930s it was over. Logging and wood exports, however, supplied a steady flow of income for people in areas like the Para district. But a single commodity increasingly eclipsed all these economic activities: bauxite.

In 1916, the Aluminum Company of America (Alcoa) came to Suriname. There had long been rumours that the material used to surface roads was bauxite, also the raw material for aluminium, and they turned out to be true. By dealing with middlemen, Alcoa had already obtained all kinds of concessions for its branch in Suriname. In December 1916, the company transferred these concessions to the Suriname Bauxite Company, which was founded to that end. After a few years of struggle, the first

Mining bauxite on Suriname Bauxite Company ground in Moengo. Collection Nationaal Museum van Wereldculturen, TM 10019737

bauxite was exported in 1922, and by 1930 over three million guilders worth of bauxite was shipped abroad – far exceeding the income from other export products. These profits decreased somewhat for a few years because of the Great Depression, but around 1935 when the global economy was in revival, bauxite increasingly started to dominate the Surinamese economy.

Several publications reproached the Dutch government for giving such expansive concessions to the Americans for so little money. They made such huge profits from the end product, aluminium, that investments in Suriname were often recouped very quickly. However, studies showed that other things were going on in the background. The United States pressured several European countries, including the Netherlands, not to harm American interests in the bauxite industry, and the Netherlands had extensive oil interests in its Dutch East India colony. The two countries made a deal: the Americans were granted access to the enormous bauxite reserves in Suriname under extremely profitable conditions, in exchange for the Americans renouncing participation in the rich oil fields near Sumatra. This way, the bauxite industry in Suriname was entirely American at first. It was only at the end of the 1930s that Dutch company Billiton would play a role in this area.

Social unrest and progress

All these economic activities did not prevent increasing numbers of people ending up on the margins of society. The global crisis of the 1930s did not bypass Suriname. Large budget cuts by the colonial government and layoffs at several companies complicated life even more for the average Surinamese citizen. Particularly the people from Paramaribo and its environs had a hard time finding employment. This impacted on small farmers, too, who found it increasingly difficult to sell their products. The situation was the ideal seedbed for uniting workers and defending the interests of people who could barely or no longer support themselves.

By 1931 the demand for change had become so pressing that trade unions took several actions. Louis Doedel played an important part in this. He used the experiences he had had gained on Curacao in 1932 when setting up the Surinamese General Workers Organisation (SAWO), uniting several different unions. The colonial government was not pleased with this joining of forces: it feared unrest in a society that had been generally peaceful until then. SAWO was banned.

In spite of this, the first half of the 1930s remained turbulent. Besides Louis Doedel, Anton de Kom also attracted the colonial government's attention in those days. According to the authorities, his ideals and actions were communist. De Kom always denied being a communist, but the suspicion remained, and apparently compounded the difficulties he experienced finding work in the decade he spent in the Netherlands. He had remained in contact with his home country throughout the years, so when he decided to return to Suriname in 1932, his supporters prepared a warm welcome. In January 1933, he and his family arrived in a colony that was in financial trouble. There was great poverty and despair, particularly among the workers in the cities. With the tensions caused by people rebelling against the misery still fresh in their mind, the colonial government took immediate measures to keep De Kom's supporters under control, but these turned out to be counterproductive. Finally, De Kom was accused of agitation and incarcerated; in May of 1933 he, his wife and their children were sent back to the Netherlands. His book *We, Slaves of Suriname* was published in 1934; in it he offers his particular view of Suriname's history, and argues that the roots of the country's problems lay in colonialism and exploitation. Only in the 1960s did the book draw the attention of a large audience, and become the classic many people regard as essential to a better understanding of Suriname's past.

Unemployed workers' demonstration in Paramaribo, 1931. Photo: Augusta Curiel. Collection Rijksmuseum Amsterdam, NG-2009-137-1

Panorama of Waterkant, Paramaribo, ca. 1925.
Photo: Augusta Curiel. Collection Rijksmuseum Amsterdam, NG-2009-41

Naturally, De Kom's deportation did not eliminate all the problems. Unemployment was rife, with no large-scale projects to get people working again. Governor Kielstra had rather strong ideas about how to solve the problems. In his view, Suriname was agricultural terrain where people, even those from the city, should work the land. Kielstra's authoritarian attitude engendered much resistance in the parliament, sometimes leading to violent clashes, but he simply used the state of emergency in 1940 to force through his ideas.

Self-development of communities

Private initiatives were also undertaken to improve the situation. One of them was the Creola project. A few men from the Creole middle class, with a certain social standing, made a few attempts at getting city Creoles, who had been struck hard by the economic crisis, back to small-scale agriculture. They were given land not far from Paramaribo. The Creola project had been thoroughly prepared, and was relatively successful in the second half of the 1930s. The proceeds enabled more families to participate in the project. The experiment ended after a few years when bauxite and the war industry offered new opportunities. The Creoles believed that education was crucial to their further development. The light-coloured members of this community adopted Western ideals, and subsequently grew to become the country's elite.

Former contract labourers who had not returned to their home countries climbed the social ladder through agriculture. Among Hindustanis the family played an important part in this process. Men, women and children were needed to work the land, which is why it is understandable that education was a secondary consideration. That the education system was mainly in the hands of the Christian communities also kept the Hindustanis from sending their children to school. They were avid supporters of public, secular schooling. Only in the 1920s, when more public schools were founded were more children sent to school: initially just the boys, and later the girls as well.

The Hindustanis did not only flourish socially, but culturally as well. Starting in 1911, several associations were founded. They represented the interests of their community, and placed great emphasis on preserving their culture. Religion played an important role in this. In 1929 and 1930, the oldest religious clubs were founded: the Sanathan Dharm, and the Arya Samaj. And their Muslim counterparts joined together as well. These were all manifestations of the fact that the Hindustani community was becoming more deeply rooted in Surinamese society. From the 1920s, more and more films were imported from India. This gave new impulses to their interest in their own culture, while several legal changes contributed as well. The Dutch Citizenship Bill of 1910 was amended in 1927, granting citizenship to Hindustanis born in Suriname, and in 1940, this population group obtained the right to marry according to their own traditions, and by their own ministers. This recognition was important for their culture.

The Javanese community underwent similar developments, albeit at a later stage. They started coming to the colony in 1890, and the flow of new workers continued until 1939. Up to 1930, they were all indentured labourers, but from 1931 on they were independent workers who usually brought their families with them. This group generally stayed in Suriname, mostly ending up in small-scale agriculture, although some of them found employment in Moengo, the city of bauxite. Though the circumstances were difficult, they persevered and progressed. Like the Hindustanis, the Javanese introduced their culture to Suriname, thus enriching their new homeland. Their small restaurants, called *warungs*, soon became a common sight. They also brought their religious traditions to the colony. The Muslim part of this group founded their own communities.

Suriname had changed fundamentally on economic, social and cultural levels in the first half of the 20th century. On the eve of the Second World War, the country slowly climbed out of the abyss it had been in. This war would prove very important for the further development of the colony.

The Second World War and the systematic approach after 1945

The Second World War and the developments that ensued were decisive for the way Suriname looked at its ability to progress. The importance of the local raw material bauxite for the American war industry is a known fact. In books, documentaries, and stories of people who remember the presence of the American soldiers, the emphasis is on producing this raw material for further processing in factories in the United States, and on the positive influence of this industry on the economical developments in Suriname. The Americans offered well-paid jobs, supply companies thrived, and the national budget could be covered by the profits the government made from this important material. Furthermore, Suriname was an important stop for American aircraft executing secret missions in South America and Africa.

American films were extremely popular at the time, the Fernandes brand introduced Coca-Cola to the Surinamese market, and the American way of life was introduced to a colony that, up to that point, had mainly been focused on the motherland. In addition, during the war the average Surinamese's self-confidence grew. Naturally, there were downsides, such as increased prostitution, growing crime rates, and power outages: Paramaribo in particular was often completely dark at night. But eventually, the country that came out of the war was very different from the one it had been when it started. Besides the economic growth, this change was also attributable to the promise made by Queen Wilhelmina during a radio speech in December 1942, broadcast from London, where the Dutch government had fled after the German's occupied the Netherlands: after the war there would be changes in the political relationship, and the colonies would have more autonomy.

Post-war developments

The bauxite industry developed further after the war. At first, production slowed down, as there was less need for aluminium. But the impending Cold War, the outbreak of the Korean War in 1950, and other tensions around the world resulted in a dramatic increase in the demand for bauxite. The Netherlands came to the conclusion that a systematic approach to Suriname's development was the best way to ensure further growth. To that purpose, the Netherlands initiated the Welfare Fund, which mainly assessed the opportunities in Suriname. They conducted aerial surveys and soil research. The country was mapped in all its dimensions to evaluate the investment prospects.

At the same time, the school system was improved, as only an educated population would be able to develop the country. Reforming the teacher's training college would yield better-qualified teachers, and a secondary school would allow for more students to move on to university. An active grants policy enabled many youngsters from various social backgrounds to attend universities in the Netherlands. This way, the number of academics grew, which made it possible to be less dependent on higher management from abroad. The locals gradually took over a number of posts.

The transformation that would exert the most influence on the further development of Suriname was a political one. The year 1949 saw the first elections based on the general right to vote. Prior to this, only men who paid a certain amount of tax, or had a certain level of education, were allowed to vote. In 1949, every adult man and woman was entitled to do so. In the period 1946 to 1949, several political parties were founded. As everything was relatively new to average Surinamese, it is no surprise that when the parties started, there was a lot of emphasis on the origins of their leaders. Parties were mainly founded to safeguard and advance the interests of particular groups, not so much to serve the country. Although in theory the parties were national, they were, in fact, not.

The new system also had its flaws. It strongly favoured the capital, at the expense of the districts and the inland. In the first parliament there were 21 seats, ten of which were assigned to Paramaribo. For those city seats, the rule 'winner takes all' applied, so whoever gained the majority in the city would receive all the seats. That party would then only have to win one seat outside its own party in the National Council, to have a majority. For a long time, the party of the Creole community, the National Party of Suriname (NPS), dominated politics in the country. Until the military coup of 1980, it was part of almost every government. The only times the party was not involved was in the periods 1955 to 1958 and 1969 to 1973. This way, the NPS, whether in coalition with other parties or not, had a say in almost every development in the country.

Another consequence of the system was that small parties came and went. Some tried their luck in the political arena; others formed coalitions that were often highly unstable. Until 1955, the NPS was the only party in the government; from 1955 there were coalition governments. This meant that representatives of other ethnic groups started to participate in the direction of the country. The political parties often had their own newspapers, or had allies in the press. Ideology was of very minor importance in Surinamese politics. It wasn't until much later that parties were founded with a clear ideology, parties that said what they stood for, and vice versa.

Institutes, infrastructure, and the economy

Post-war development included creating the institutes that had to ensure plans were made and executed. The Planning Office of Suriname was in charge of these tasks. This Office made a significant contribution to the first Ten-Year Plan, which began in 1954.

To gain a better insight into the population's development, the government regularly carried out censuses after the Second World War: in 1950, 1964, and 1971. Particularly interesting was the birth rate among descendants of the Asian contract labourers: after the war, that group grew to form over 50 per cent of the total population. Thanks to improved accessibility to the hinterland, censuses could be carried out there as well, which made it possible to accurately map the descendants of the freed slaves who had found their freedom in the woods. The original inhabitants of Suriname were counted as well. Data about family situations and incomes were vital to drawing up specific plans for the country's development, the idea being: the better the plans, the faster the development. The education system benefitted from this data too: new secondary schools were built such as the Lyceum in 1965, and in 1968, the country got its first university. The various teachers training courses in Suriname were merged into the Teacher's Education Institute.

Infrastructural works, such as the construction of roads, made the country more accessible. The entire coastal area was opened up, and thanks to the building of small airports in the interior, the inlanders had better access to medical care and education. The largest project, executed in the 1960s, was the construction of the Afobaka Dam for the generation of hydroelectric power for the bauxite industry. Part of the land of Upper Suriname was turned into a lake, the Brokopondo Reservoir, which would supply energy for the Alcoa factory. The hydroelectric power station and the factory came online in 1965. Suriname, as one of the very few developing countries, now had a fully integrated aluminium industry: the extraction of bauxite, processing it into alumina, melting it down to aluminium – from that point on, everything was done in Suriname. This gave the economy an enormous boost. However, the Surinamese workers who were employed in the construction of the dam, the power station and the factory, lost their jobs. Some of the immigration to the Netherlands at the end of the 1960s can be explained by the increase in unemployment when this project was completed.

The downside to this large project was that Suriname more than ever became dependent on a single product and industry, which moreover was almost completely owned by a foreign corporation. During the 1950s, local attempts to finance the dam and reservoir had failed. Some foreign banks had been willing to finance the projects, as prospects for the Surinamese bauxite industry were excellent, but the Netherlands refused to act as guarantor for the loan. There have been several explanations for this refusal. For example, the Netherlands did not see the need for such a large project in

The Afobaka Dam on the Suriname River at Brokopondo, sealed in 1964.
Collection Nationaal Museum van Wereldculturen TM 20007653

Harvesting rice mechanically on the Prince Bernhard polder, 1951.
Collection Nationaal Museum van Wereldculturen, TM 10033018

Suriname, and furthermore the motherland had its own aluminium industry and was not keen on any competition coming from Suriname. Whatever the reasons, Suriname had an important industry but it wasn't in local hands. It contributed greatly to the economy, but, comparatively speaking, it did not provide many jobs. And that was exactly what a growing population needed.

Rice production was another economic activity. In the 1960s, Suriname was renowned when it came to the development of rice varieties. Wageningen was famous for experiments that had produced high-quality strains. Fishing and shrimp exports flourished as well. The banana industry was once more on the rise, and this time it remained steady, proving to be important not only for employment, but also for export. Timber, one of the traditional export products, still found new clients in the Caribbean and parts of South America. Bruynzeel Suriname Timber Company's experiments with kit homes (prefabricated houses that were easy to erect) were quite successful. These kits were even sold throughout the entire region. These sectors all provided jobs. Finally, there was a lot of work to be found in the civil service, which was increasingly used to provide jobs without there being enough actual work.

The rise of the trade unions

Surinamese society also changed in other ways during the 1960s. The rise of the trade unions, defending the interests of their members ever more articulately, was remarkable. Not only did the unions' social influence grow, but they also began to manifest politically. At first this close alliance benefitted the workers, because they were now able to force the government to distribute more provisions and facilities. However, there were a few negative aspects as well. Once in power, former union leaders were not always willing to heed those who had supported their rise. Moreover, the interests of the government in place were served better than those of union members. This conflict of interests made it difficult to stay objective. For example, well-known politician Johan Pengel was prime minister and chairman of a trade union federation for years. Eventually, when he had to choose, he chose politics. Ironically, in the late 1960s it was the trade unions that brought him down.

The unions have been a political power to be reckoned with ever since. In the years 1969 to 1973, when unemployment rates were high in Suriname, they caused a lot of problems for the Sedney/Lachmon government. After the 1973 elections, the most important unions became part of the government. Some of the representatives became government Ministers and Secretaries of State; the rest went to the Estates of Suriname. It was during this term, from 1973 to 1977, that Suriname became independent, a transition that was accompanied by a lot of unrest and ethnic tension. Many left the country, fearing that the situation would spin out of control after the Dutch departed. It did not, and eventually independence was established peacefully. The political differences between the parties who had voted for and against independence turned out to be less pronounced than many had thought. The party leaders, Jagernath Lachmon and Henck Arron, were reconciled. The Dutch promise of a large amount of development aid contributed to the orderly completion of the process, as had the agreement that for the next five years, Surinamese citizens could still migrate to the Netherlands without hindrance.

Suriname after independence

In the years between 1975 and the military coup in February 1980, a portion of the Dutch development aid was invested in the economy and in socio-cultural projects. A lot of money became available, but a large proportion of it went straight back to the former motherland, as virtually all commissions for the large infrastructural projects went to Dutch companies. Moreover, much of the knowledge came from the Netherlands, as did many of the materials. Suriname thus realised its independence in a relatively peaceful way and had a lot of money to spend, but no real vision. There was a Multi-Annual Development Plan and projects were funded based on that plan, but there was a lot of social discontent. This was reflected in the mass migration to the Netherlands in the years 1978 and 1979: people were seeking more security, before it would become impossible in 1980. So, a mere five years after the 1974/75 exodus, there was a second one.

The reasons for the people's discontent were legion. Although a lot of money was invested in large projects, especially in the west of Suriname, the population hardly noticed any results. Frustrations about practical issues such as the lack of drinking water did not make things easier. Meanwhile, political tensions rose when the coalition government's majority in the Estates of Suriname declined to a single seat (the coalition had 20 seats, the opposition 19), and one of the coalition members passed away. At that point, both the coalition and the opposition had 19 seats in the Estates, and a standoff developed around the question of whether the remaining 19 members could call for an assembly to admit a new, 20th member. After months of political tussle, it was decided to admit the new member, most of all because it was almost time for elections. The army was also a subject of discussion. Some wanted to create a military trade union, following the Dutch example, but the government opposed the idea. The tensions erupted in a military coup on 25 February 1980. Suriname had entered a new phase.

The 1980s

The period between 1980 and 1987 was very eventful in Suriname. It is difficult to write a balanced narrative about that time: the events are still too fresh, and most of those involved are still alive. It is, however, not impossible, if it is done with the same accuracy with which events from thousands of years ago have been described, while remembering that there is no such thing as neutral historiography. Every writer has to select what he or she does or doesn't write down, leading to the inevitable conclusion that no form of historiography is free of bias. Especially in this case, when we are talking about a description of a time the author experienced firsthand.

There was a tangible sense of relief among the population after the coup, but at the same time there was uncertainty about what the military council intended for the country. There was a civilian government with only a few military members, which was promising. But further tensions arose when it became evident that there were different camps within the army that were not on the same wavelength. Furthermore, while there was a civilian government, it was quite obvious that the really important decisions were being made, or at least approved, elsewhere. This made for a lasting competence dispute between civilians and the military.

The first major rift came in August 1980, when the constitution ratified after independence in 1975 was suspended, only to disappear completely shortly thereafter. A second major crisis occurred in March 1982, with a failed attempt within the army itself to seize power from the perpetrators of the 1980 coup. Eventually, the execution of the coup leaders and fifteen opponents from several sections of the population – the latter known as the December Murders of 1982 – led to a complete social standstill. Fear is never a good way to maintain a regime, mostly because few people will be willing to support any new initiative in such a situation.

At the same time, the global economic crisis in the 1980s made it hard for Suriname to keep its head above water. The bauxite industry was in deep trouble, as global prices had declined significantly. The Surinamese currency was devalued as well, which led to a reduction in consumption. Furthermore, foreign currency reserves were almost non-existent, severely affecting imports. Empty shop shelves became a common sight in the country. After the December Murders, the Dutch government ceased paying Suriname the development aid it had agreed to at the time of independence. Current projects had to be put on hold, which made for even more economic stagnation and unemployment.

The situation in Suriname after 1982 was an ideal seedbed for groups outside the country to campaign against the military regime. As is often the case with newly independent nations, opposition to the rulers does not only start outside the national borders, but inside as well. In the east of the country, young Maroons took up arms, leading to the Suriname Interior War, which lasted until 1992. The social, socio-economic and political consequences were substantial, and several massacres on both sides made for an extra grim atmosphere.

The era of re-democratisation

Against all odds, a re-democratisation process started. A new constitution was ratified in the National Assembly, which was installed in 1980, replacing the Parliament of the Republic of Suriname. It paved the way for the first free and general elections in ten years. After a period of military dominance, Suriname once again installed a fully elected civilian government in 1987. This government was a coalition of old political parties that were in power before the coup. There was a new party associated with the military, the National Democratic Party (NDP), but it had not yet been able to make a political stand. This would change later.

Currency depreciation in the 1980s and 1990s was clearly evident in the notes with three zeros. Private collection

The authorities wanted to revive the collapsed economy, but lacked the means. Meanwhile, the Suriname Internal War continued, over which they hardly had any control. They had counted on the resumption of Dutch development aid, but the Dutch felt that the situation in the country had changed such that the aid it provided was no longer merely a matter of course. The relationship between the two became a painful game of demands on one side and refusal to fulfil them on the other.

The government and the army struggled to get along after 1987. Military officials who have been at the centre of power in a country do not usually sit and watch while their privileges are taken away from them, and Suriname was no exception. The government signed a peace treaty with the Jungle Commando – as the inland fighters of the guerrilla war called themselves – but the army did not agree. The treaty failed. After many negotiations between the several parties, and with foreign help, peace was finally concluded in 1992.

However, that was not the end of the vicissitudes between the civilian government and the military authorities. In 1990 it had become clear that both parties were unable to collaborate. In December that year, the government was sent home. The same parties returned to power after elections a year later, albeit with a small majority. The new government decided to dismiss several high-ranking officials who had been embroiled

Members of Ronnie Brunswijk's Jungle Commando with *obla* (charmed necklaces, bracelets, etc.), which supposedly protected them from the National Army, 1987. In the middle advisor and spokesperson Frits Hirschland. Private collection

in the 1980 coup. A new leadership was installed, and gradually the dominance of the military decreased.

Former coup participants then became increasingly involved with politics. They saw that the old parties were losing a lot of goodwill among the Surinamese people. Besides, the electorate was becoming younger: people could vote from the age of 18 after 1987. That generation could scarcely remember the violent, early days of the coup, and the political murders of December 1982 meant less to them on an emotional level. That is how the advance of the NDP started.

Economic recovery

The country's economy started showing signs of recovery in the final decade of the 20th century. Prices on the global commodities market were rising, and an oil industry had started to develop in Suriname. The Netherlands had tentatively started financing Surinamese projects again. Those were all promising signs that Suriname might be climbing out of its economic abyss.

That did not mean the population benefitted from the recovery directly, and the results at the 1996 elections showed as much. Although a coalition government had actually finished its constitutional five-year term for the first time since 1980, after the elections there was a division, which provided an opportunity for military-linked civilians to form a new government. The army was once again in power, though this time they were democratically elected.

It would not be a happy return: the party's internal differences and those with the traditional parties turned out to be so unbridgeable that snap elections had to be called. Nevertheless, this government did one very important thing between 1996 and 2000: it built a bridge over the Suriname River, so now a permanent road linked east and west. It was a very old wish come true for many, and the Commewijne district benefitted greatly from it. The inhabitants could travel to Paramaribo much faster now, and were no longer dependent on a boat service that could be cancelled due to technical or other problems. The district was flooded with new people who could now live there without running the risk of being delayed while travelling to their jobs in the city.

Regional integration and further growth

Not only the bridge brought social change – a new awareness of the importance of integration in the region did as well. In 1995, Suriname became a full member of the Caribbean Community (Caricom), and as a result, consumers and producers soon noticed that supermarket shelves were filling up with foreign drinks and other products. Everyone realised that they could benefit from this new arrangement and sell their products to a wider market than just the local one. In reality, it took some time for this to actually happen. The more developed Republic of Trinidad and Tobago became an important trading partner. The oil and gas industry had brought the twin-island country wealth, which is why its people had money to spend.

In the meantime, Suriname was well on its way with its own oil industry. After 1980 the idea of taking more initiatives to develop the country from within, to have faith in the country's own abilities, had taken root. Setting up a petroleum industry was one of those initiatives. Staatsolie Maatschappij Suriname N.V. (State Oil Company of Suriname N.V.), the national oil company founded in December 1980, was involved in all aspects of the industry: exploitation, extraction, processing and distribution. The company accumulated quite a lot of expertise, and when necessary it bought in external expertise that it could also apply in the future. Several parties claimed responsibility for State Oil's success. What is certain is that successive governments were very happy with the yearly dividends of this fully Surinamese state company: they could now spend money on things they hadn't had the means for in the past.

Though the oil industry's business model could not yet be transposed onto other sectors, there were more success stories. The gold reserves that had been so lucrative at the end of the 19th century were even more so at the start of the 21st. Individual gold prospectors and large foreign companies made a lot of money from gold, but so did the government and part of the population. It was this, and the revenues from the oil industry that largely protected Suriname from the global recession in the early 21st century. The gold sites were mostly in the Maroon regions, and they participated *en masse* in exploiting the reserves, often in collaboration with Brazilians, who provided the necessary expertise. The gold mining was generally environmentally unfriendly: a lot of mercury was used in the process. The activities also led to clashes between Maroons and large foreign corporations who received large concessions, which sometimes went straight through the Maroon's residential areas.

A new political century

On a political level, the first decade of the 21st century brought yet more changes. The group that was associated with the military regime turned out to be less stable than thought. The trade unions could not accept the devastating effects the economic decline had on the workers, which led to demonstrations, a further loss of support for the government, and finally snap elections in 2000. The traditional parties won. The economy – and its recovery – dominated the 2000–2005 term. The Surinamese dollar replaced the guilder, so as to better fit in with the economy of the region, and several zeros were conveniently eliminated in the process: instead of paying many thousands for a product, now you paid a few tenners.

During the 2005 elections, to have a majority the traditional parties had to include a coalition of Maroon parties in their team. For the first time, this sector of the Surinamese population became part of the government. This government could benefit from the high commodity prices, and from the remainder of the Dutch development aid agreed to in 1975. But still, the problem remained that the population did not immediately see their living standards improve because of the positive macro-economical developments. Social services were minimal, and often did not reach the people who needed them the most. In the meantime, support for the traditional parties declined further, while the NDP was growing in popularity. It was only a matter of

Maroon prospector.
Photo: Toon Fey

time before the latter would democratically rise to power. At the 2010 elections, the traditional parties had to face the consequences: the NDP coalition became the largest.

The man most associated with the 1980 coup, Desiré Bouterse, was elected president, and a broad coalition government was formed. Now, Bouterse found out to his cost what it meant to be in power alongside many different parties. His proposal that several important partners within the government lacked a development vision not only characterised former governments, but his too. It became a laborious government term, with many Cabinet reshuffles. For the first two years, this Cabinet had ample money at its disposal, thanks to the favourable commodity prices, but in spite of that developing a clear policy proved arduous. The social agreement the NDP had made with the people on the eve of the elections did bring improvements in welfare provisions, but the question remains of whether there is enough money to guarantee those in the long run. The 21st century offers many opportunities for Suriname to not only progress through the exploitation of raw materials, but most of all through the further development of the country's human potential. That is a much better guarantee for ongoing progress.

Towards the future

Since the abolition of slavery in 1863, Suriname has developed from a Dutch colony to an independent nation that progresses by falling over and picking itself up again. In the second decade of the 21st century, the country's full potential on a number of levels has yet to be reached. The various communities have had room to develop, but that did not happen at the same pace for everyone, and not always without problems. There have been ethnic tensions, but far less than in other (Caribbean) countries, and they have not permanently divided the society. The economy has grown, but also only in part, and not always in a sustainable way. Politics and parliament developed from a colonial setup when only a limited group was allowed to vote, to the present-day National Assembly and its parties – important institutions in the society, which are prescribed by the voting regulations. A colonial society has become a mature society that, while it has not always been able to choose a problem-free development path, is trying to find its way between the many obstacles in this world in a relatively peaceful way.

The swearing in of Ronnie Brunswijk as a member of the Surinamese parliament. Photo: *Dagblad Suriname*

Literature

Benjamins, H.D. & J.F. Snelleman (eds.), *Encyclopaedie van Nederlandsch West-Indië*. Amsterdam: S. Emmering, 1981. (Unrevised edition of 1914–17)

Bruijning, C. & J. Voorhoeve (eds.), *Encyclopedie van Suriname*. Amsterdam: Elsevier, 1977.

Buddingh', Hans, *Geschiedenis van Suriname*. Amsterdam: Nieuw Amsterdam/NRC Boeken, 2012.

Egger, Jerome (ed.), *Ontwaakt en ontwikkelt U: Creolen na de afschaffing van de slavernij 1863-1940*. Paramaribo: Institute for Social Science Research, 2013.

Gobardhan-Rambocus, Lila, *Onderwijs als sleutel tot maatschappelijke vooruitgang: Een taal- en onderwijsgeschiedenis van Suriname*. Zutphen: Walburg Pers, 2001.

Hassankhan, Maurits, Lila Gobardhan-Rambocus & Jerry Egger (eds.), *De erfenis van de slavernij*. Paramaribo: Anton de Kom University of Suriname, 1995.

Heilbron, Waldo, *Kleine Boeren in de schaduw van de plantage: De politieke ekonomie van de na-slavernijperiode in Suriname*. Paramaribo/Amsterdam, 1982. (Dissertation)

Hira, Sandew, *Van Priary tot en met De Kom: De geschiedenis van het verzet in Suriname, 1630-1940*. Rotterdam: Futile, 1983.

Lier, Rudolf van, *Samenleving in een grensgebied: Een sociaalhistorische studie van Suriname*. Third revised edition. Amsterdam: S. Emmering, 1977.

Polak, J.A., *Historisch overzicht van de goudindustrie in Suriname*. The Hague: Martinus Nijhoff, 1908.

Ramsoedh, Hans, *Suriname 1933-1944: Koloniale politiek en beleid onder gouverneur Kielstra*. Delft: Eburon, 1990.

Sack, J., *De Balata-industrie in Suriname*. Paramaribo, 1909.

Scholtens, Ben, *Louis Doedel: Surinaamse vakbondsleider van het eerste uur. Een bronnenpublicatie*. Paramaribo: Anton de Kom University of Suriname, 1987.

Scholtens, Ben, *Opkomende arbeidersbeweging in Suriname: Doedel, Liesdek, De Sanders, De Kom en de werklozenonrust 1931-1933*. Nijmegen: Transculturele Uitgeverij Masusa, 1986.

Struycken, C.A.J. & J.W. Gonggrijp, *Het balata vraagstuk in Suriname*. Paramaribo: J.H. Oliviera, 1912.

Traa, A. van, *Suriname 1900-1940*. Deventer: Uitgeverij W. van Hoe, 1946.

Wieringen, A.G. van, et al., *Rapport betreffende het kleinbedrijf in de goudindustrie in de kolonie Suriname*. The Hague: F.J. Belinfante (1906).

Willemsen, Glenn, *Dagen van gejuich en gejubel: Viering en herdenking van de afschaffing van de slavernij in Nederland, Suriname en de Nederlandse Antillen*. The Hague/Amsterdam: Amrit/Ninsee, 2006.

Wix, L., *De Balata-industrie van Nickerie*. Nieuw Nickerie: Cultural Centre Nickerie (1979).

Wolff, H., *Historisch overzicht over Suriname 1613-1934*. The Hague: Self published, 1934.

Jerome Egger is a lecturer at the Anton de Kom University of Suriname and is editor of the journal *Hisher Tori*, published by the university's Institute for Social Science Research (IMWO).

Mining in Suriname

Its past, present and future

Glenn Gemerts

Mining, or the extraction of minerals by moving earth dates back to prehistoric times, when people began exploiting natural resources, including mineral deposits, to provide for their survival and development. The earliest form of mining in Suriname was the exploitation of clay around the seventeenth century. In this chapter we examine the history of mining in Suriname and it future potential.

A brief history of mining in Suriname, some highlights

Gold

Gold mining in Suriname began in the last decades of the nineteenth century. This sector was strongly encouraged during the tenure of Governor Van Sypesteyn, from 1873 to 1882, not only to develop it further, but also to improve relations with the inland inhabitants. Exploration and exploitation activities steadily increased at that time, but this well-ordered, mechanised gold mining lasted only a few years, after which it failed due to lack of exploration, insufficient knowledge of gold mineralisation, mismanagement, speculation, and diseases such as malaria.

Small-scale gold mining began around 1900. Holders of larger concessions (mining rights) leased parts of their land to individual prospectors, nicknamed *'porknokkers'*, for an agreed percentage of the proceeds. Subsequently, gold production increased dramatically, and even rose above production levels achieved with the short-lived mechanised gold mining. Small-scale gold mining activities occurred on land and in rivers. Known sites were Gross Rosebel, Benz Village, Sarakreek and Lawa River. In 1903 the Dutch colonial government decided to stimulate the gold industry by constructing a railway line from Paramaribo to the gold fields: along the Lawa River via Kwakugron, Kabel and Dam on the Sarakreek. But when gold production declined again and surveys in the Lawa region proved to be disappointing, it was decided in 1912 not to construct the railway line from Dam to the Lawa Gold Fields after all.

Only in the 1980s did interest in small-scale gold mining resurge. This was seen as a potential source of employment and income – especially for the interior peoples – and as a catalyst for rural development. To address this, in 1981 the Minister of Natural Resources and Energy proposed that the government adopt explicit regulations relating

Small-scale gold mining.
Photo: Marco de Nood

to small-scale gold mining. The Mining Code, which was formulated in 1986, also paid attention to the negative consequences and therefore formulated unambiguous deterrents. Small-scale gold mining was confined to areas designated for that purpose by the government.

The Suriname Interior War (1986–1992) and the arrival of large numbers of Brazilian gold miners *(garimpeiros)* resulted in an increase in the production of gold. The intensive scale of the work – by *garimpeiros* and the local population, legal and illegal, along with the significant misuse of mercury that was not recovered – led to the siltation of rivers and creeks. Other consequences of the gold industry include the serious disruption of the physical landscape (mining here creates enormous craters), social conflict and crime. The economic benefits of small-scale gold mining remains significant, but so does the seriousness of the social and environmental consequences.

Developing large-scale gold mining in Suriname has been considerably more difficult. Between 1974 and 1977, the government surveyed for gold in the Gross-Rosebel region in a joint venture with the Canadian gold mining company Placer Dome. However, the results were insignificant. In 1979 the State Mining Corporation, N.V. Grassalco,

Placer gold mining in Suriname, ca. 1925. Photo: Augusta Curiel. Collection Nationaal Museum van Wereldculturen, TM 60006384

Iamgold's Rosebel operation.
Photo: Marco de Nood

was awarded an exploration permit. A 1984 feasibility study indicated that economic exploitation of the gold deposits to a depth of ten metres was possible, but funding could not be raised for this project.

In April 1994, the government signed a mineral agreement with Golden Star Resources and N.V. Grassalco for further exploration and the exploitation of the gold in the Gross-Rosebel region. However, in the ensuing period the price of gold on the world market fell dramatically below the level used in the feasibility study. The conditions relating to financing gold mining projects were subsequently tightened, and the mineral agreement had to be amended in 2003. In May 2002 Cambior Inc. took over Golden Star Resources' share of the company in Suriname. On 14 April 2004 the mine at Rosebel was opened, officially marking the beginning of large-scale industrial gold mining in Suriname. In November 2006, Iamgold Corporation took over all the interests of Cambior Inc.

SBM bauxite mine in Moengo, 1922.
Nationaal Museum van Wereldculturen, TM 10019711

Bauxite

In 1916, a subsidiary of the Aluminum Company of America (Alcoa), the Suriname Bauxite Company (later called Suralco LLC), began prospecting for bauxite in Moengo and then with its exploitation. Bauxite exports began around 1922. Twenty years later, in 1942, the N.V. Billiton Maatschappij Suriname, as a subsidiary of N.V. Billiton Maatschappij, started mining bauxite in Onverdacht, near Smalkalden. This bauxite was also exported.

In the late 1950s it started to become evident that Suriname would accrue more profits if the raw material was processed into alumina and aluminium locally. On 4 February 1957 the government of Suriname and Alcoa signed a Letter of Intent: Alcoa would build an aluminium smelter in Suriname in exchange for new bauxite concessions in the country and a dam for generating energy for the smelter. The deal fell through, however, because of opposition from the Dutch government, which refused to guarantee the loan from the World Bank that was necessary to construct the dam. But on 27 January 1958 the Brokopondo Agreement between the government of Suriname and Suralco could still be signed: Alcoa agreed to cover the cost of constructing the dam. It was completed in 1964, and 1965 saw the completion of a hydroelectric power plant generating 189 megawatts, an aluminium smelter with a capacity of 60,000 tons per year, and an alumina refinery with an annual capacity of 650,000 tonnes. Suralco also received bauxite-prospecting concessions that were valid until 2032.

The Geological Mining Service

Although mining played an important role in Suriname's economy from the nineteenth century, the sector did not have a dedicated government department until the 1940s. On 14 December 1943 the decision was taken to appoint a representative from the Department of Social and Economic Affairs who would oversee the implementation of the provisions of the Mineral Resources Regulation: mining engineer H. Schols. In 1949 the name of his department was changed into the Geological Mining Service (GMD), part of the Department of Economic Affairs. In 1958, the GMD became part of the Ministry of Development, now called the Ministry of Natural Resources.

At its formation the GMD was assigned four responsibilities: making geological maps; inventorising mineral resources; advising the Minister on mining legislation, exploration permits-and concessions; and monitoring the activities of third parties resulting from these (mine inspections), and providing services to others in the field of geological reconnaissance and mining inventory.

Railway line in West Suriname (Bakhuis-Apoera). Photo: Roy Tjin

Partly thanks to Operation Grasshopper (1959–62), which involved constructing airstrips in the interior, geological surveys of Surinamese territory were easily and accurately performed during the 1960s and 1970s. One of the main accomplishments of this geological fieldwork was the creation of a geological map of Suriname in 1977.

Thanks to research conducted by the Geological and Mining Service, bauxite deposits were discovered in the Bakhuis region in West Suriname the 1960s. To exploit these and further develop West Suriname, the State mining company N.V. Grassalco was founded in 1971. That same year Grassalco entered into a joint venture with Reynolds Suriname Mines Ltd., but differences of opinion led to this cooperation being terminated a mere three years later, after which Grassalco continued independently. To bring bauxite mining in this region up to speed, construction of a 72-kilometre-long railway line from Bakhuis to Apoera commenced in 1976.

The first drilling at Dankbaarheid in the Saramacca district, 1982.
Photo: State Oil

The 45 years since the late 1960s have seen a great deal of philosophising about the development of an integrated aluminium industry in West Suriname, including a hydropower generating plant. Apoera was predestined to become an industrial hub and one of the motors of the Surinamese economy. However, various attempts by both the government and a number of multinationals to develop the bauxite reserves in West Suriname have so far not led to them being exploited.

Based on the idea that bauxite was the mainstay of the Surinamese economy, the Bauxite Institute of Suriname (BIS) was established in 1981. To ensure its survival, attention had to be paid to maintaining and expanding the bauxite industry, obtaining a fair share of the revenues from bauxite and its derivatives, and the acquisition of specialised knowledge relating to the industry. On its foundation BIS was given two main tasks: on the one hand, to support the government's bauxite policy with advice, policy formation and cooperating in its implementation, and on the other hand the collection and processing of data about the bauxite industry.

Oil

Suriname developed its own oil industry from the beginning of the 1980s. The then Oil Commission negotiated an oil agreement between the yet to be established Staatsolie Maatschappij (State Oil Company) and Gulf Oil Corporation to exploit a portion of Suriname's territorial waters. As a consequence, in December 1980, the Staatsolie Maatschappij Suriname N.V. (State Oil Company of Suriname N.V.) was established. With technical assistance from Gulf Oil a start was made the following year with the production of crude oil in the Tambaredjo region in Saramacca. Gradually State Oil grew into a fully integrated oil company active in the field of exploration (in offshore areas, in collaboration with others), extraction, transportation, sales, refining and distribution. In the meantime, electricity generation has also become part of its activities. In addition to its contributions to the state coffers and employment (especially people with higher education), other important merits of State Oil include the development of management and other skills, as well as techniques for the oil industry.

The State Oil refinery.
Photo: State Oil

The significance of mining for the economy

Suriname's economy is dominated by the mining industry, which produces the lion's share of export earnings and constitutes a significant portion of the government's income. The production focuses on bauxite, gold, oil, and – to a lesser extent – construction materials.

Bauxite

Currently the only bauxite and alumina producer in Suriname is Suralco, which since 1995 has been involved in a joint venture with Australian company, Alumina Ltd. Until August 2009, Suralco also had a partnership with N.V. Billiton Maatschappij Suriname, in which Billiton mined bauxite and Suralco processed it into alumina. However, in 2008 Billiton announced that it intended to cease working on the bauxite project in the Bakhuis region and left Suriname a year later.

Figures 1 and 2 show the production and export of bauxite and alumina by quantity and value. The decline in production and exports over the years is clearly evident.

Figure 1a. Bauxite Production, 2004–12
Source: UNCTAD Global Commodities Forum, Geneva–Switserland, 2014

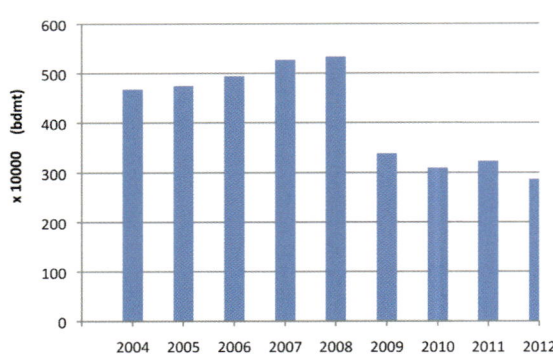

Figure 1b. Alumina Production, 2004–12
Source: UNCTAD Global Commodities Forum, Geneva–Switserland, 2014

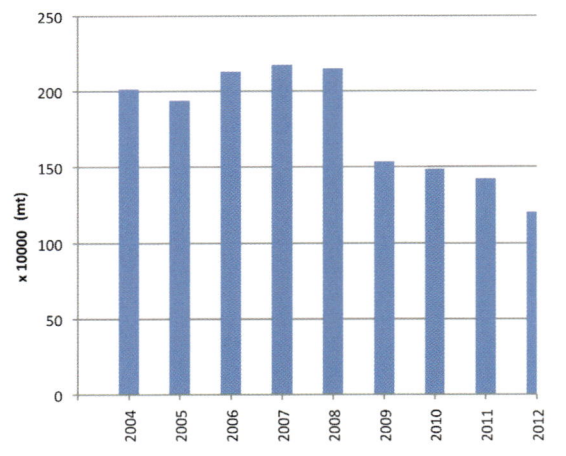

Figure 2a. Alumina exports (quantities)
Source: UNCTAD Global Commodities Forum, Geneva–Switserland, 2014

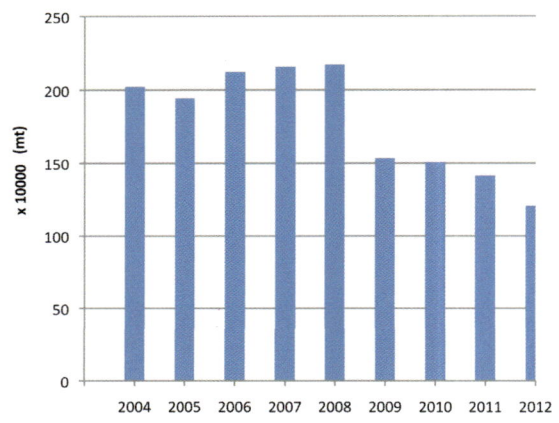

Figure 2b. Alumina exports (value)
Source: UNCTAD Global Commodities Forum, Geneva–Switserland, 2014

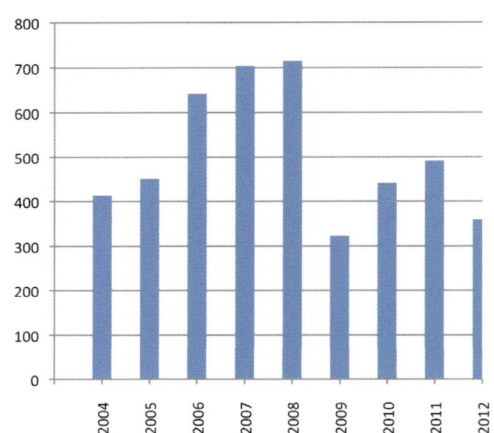

Gold

Gold is produced on a large scale by Rosebel Gold Mines N.V., of which Iamgold holds 95 per cent of the shares and the Surinamese government 5 per cent. Legal as well as illegal small-scale gold miners comprise the so-called informal sector. However, what is referred to as small-scale mining is certainly not an unsophisticated trade, given the high amounts spent on equipment such as excavators, bulldozers, high-pressure pumps, four-wheel drives, infrastructure and other costly forms of transportation, and in particular the amount of earth that is moved.

Table 1 shows that as the global price of gold increases, so does its production, in both small (SsM) and large-scale mining (LsM). The contribution of small-scale gold mining to the total is impressive.

Table 1 Gold – buy-out and production in Suriname, 1997–2012

(*Estimates based on GsM production and KsM buy-out figures*)

Year	Gold production in kgs	GsM production in kg	KsM production in kg	Average price p/g/y (US$)	Value GsM (US$ x1000)	Value KsM (US$ x1000)	Total value (US$ x 1000)
1998	6478		6478	9.50		61541	61541
1999	7004		7004	9.00		63036	63036
2000	6552		6552	9.00		58968	58968
2001	4605		4605	8.70		40064	40064
2002	2532		2532	10.00		25320	25320
2003	11559		11559	11.70		135240	135240
2004	21539	8800	12739	13.20	116160	168155	284315
2005	22644	10977	1167	14.29	156861	166721	323583
2006	21490	9678	11812	19.40	187753	229153	416906
2007	22877	8874	14003	22.36	198423	313107	511530
2008	26420	9937	16483	28.03	278534	462018	740552
2009	29734	13247	16487	31.26	414101	515384	929485
2010	31517	12701	18816	39.38	500165	740974	1241139
2011	31571	12379	19192	50.54	625635	969964	1595599
2012	32815	11880	20935	53.69	637837	1124000	1761837

Only the registered SsM purchases are included in the table. Export figures were available for the years 2010 and 2011. When it is sold SsM gold is not pure. Buyers remove some of the mercury waste it contains by burning. This can reduce the weight of the gold offered for buy-out by a few per cent. Some metals, such as silver and copper, remain in the gold and are removed during refining. To obtain a better estimate the KsM figures would have to be adjusted downwards by a few per cent.

Part of the SsM gold bought in Suriname comes from French Guiana and possibly also from Guyana. Estimating this quantity is difficult. Detailed research at the gold mining areas in Suriname would clarify the statistics.

LsM gold produced in Suriname is purer than SsM gold, but this is also refined abroad, which means the GsM figures should be reduced by a few per cent too.

Export figures are lower than the actual buyout figures due to delays in exports at the end of the year.

Oil

The State Oil Company of Suriname N.V. is the sole producer of petroleum and petroleum products in Suriname. The production of crude oil by State Oil is shown in Figure 3; this level has remained the same for the past few years.

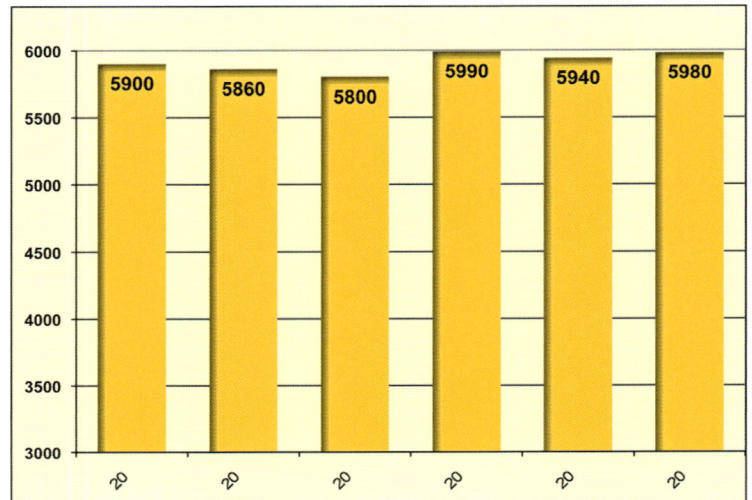

Figure 3. Crude oil production, 2008–13 (x 1000 barrels)
Source: State Oil

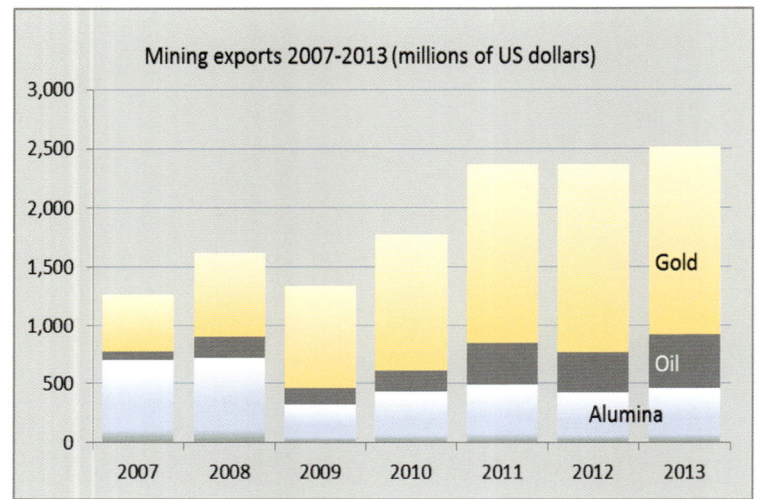

Figure 4. Exports of mining products, 2007–13
Source: The Central Bank of Suriname

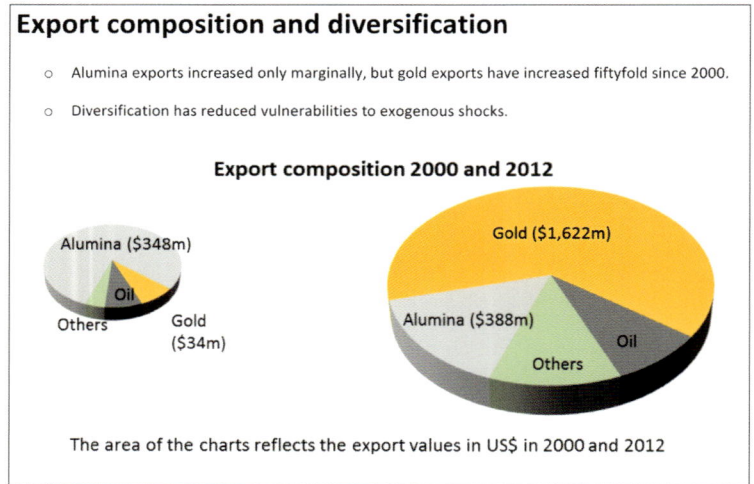

Figure 5. Exports of mining products
Source: The Central Bank of Suriname

Exports of bauxite, gold and oil

The exports of the three main mining products are shown in Figures 4 and 5. Noteworthy are the decrease in alumina exports and the increase in oil and gold exports. The contribution of these mining products to the Surinamese economy is disproportionate: less than 9 per cent of the population works in these industries, yet they account for approximately 40 per cent of the national income, over 80 per cent of net foreign exchange earnings, and about 40 per cent of state revenues.

Building materials

The production of building materials is done by individuals and companies. Table 2 shows the state revenue from the construction sector by type of building material. The State earns royalties on this trade. This does not represent the value of the materials produced, but does enable the volume produced to be deduced from the amounts.

Table 2. Income of the Surinamese government from royalties on sales of building materials, 2010–13

Construction material	2010	2011	2012	2013
Fill sand	16230.04	13438.30	292276.70	7925.65
Savannah sand	4634.60	7743.20	7758.00	880.95
Aggregate sand	26372.54	67566.66	40218.24	49295.06
Clay	0.00	0.00	0.00	0.00
Gravel	12135.95	29873.15	30214.15	25564.38
Shells	2799.60	5426.80	5298.20	2324.80
Road metal	118415.50	105550.68	22829.20	110415.53
Natural stone	1600.00	0.00	0.00	0.00
Kaolin	0.00	0.00	800.00	0.00
Laterite	2295.60	4596.40	1143.20	0.00
Total (SRD)	184483.83	234195.19	400537.69	196406.37

Source: Geological Mining Service (GMD), Database Dept., 11 July 2014

Factors that could influence the development of mineral resources

Minerals in general and metals in particular have specific features and applications such that they play a vital role in daily life and in the economic development of a region or country. They form the basis of our industrialised society. To meet the growing demand for mineral resources, companies seek these natural resources across the globe. For countries with potential mineral resources a thorough knowledge of the geological conditions in which deposits can occur is of paramount importance.

Suriname's geology

To establish which minerals – besides those already known – could possibly be recovered under favourable circumstances, and where they occur, a thorough investigation of Suriname's geology is required. Suriname is part of a geological entity called the Guiana Shield. A shield is a segment of the continental crust that has little relief and has been tectonically stable for many millions of years. The Guiana Shield has an area of roughly 1,000,000 square kilometres and underlies French Guyana, Suriname, Guyana and parts of northern Brazil, eastern Venezuela and eastern Colombia.

Relatively little is known about the geology of this area. This is because the dense vegetation, the deep weathering of the rocks and the thick laterite caps make it very difficult for geologists to study it with the naked eye. It is only with indirect methods such as geophysical measurements, satellite imagery and other remote sensing techniques that the substrate can be better mapped. Findings show that in addition to the already known mineral resources in the Guiana Shield, there are also commercially viable quantities of kaolin, manganese, chrome, diamond, tin, niobium, thorium, and minerals with rare earth elements. The mineral production of neighbouring countries could also be indicators: French Guyana exploits sand, clay, crushed stone, gold, niobium and tantalum; and Guyana bauxite, gold, diamonds and construction materials.

Figure 6. The Guiana Shield
Source: bing.com/images

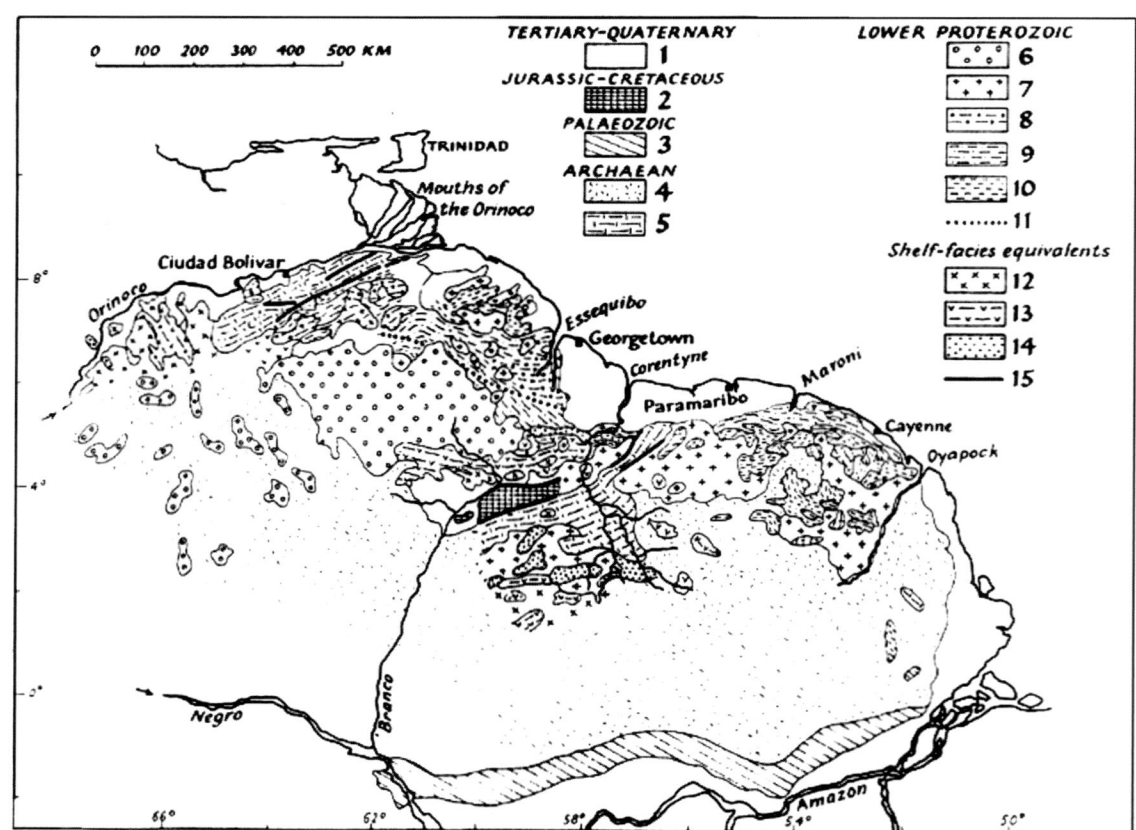

Although it could be tentatively stated that the prospects for Surinamese mineral production are not inauspicious as long as there is a favourable demand and price on the world market, for the actual realisation of further exploration and exploitation investors have to be involved. Obviously, the presence of relatively cheap energy and a good infrastructure will make Suriname interesting for investors. But more is needed to get them on board.

A dramatic leap forward has to occur in the area of knowhow. The geological map of Suriname is already 35 years old. In the meantime, neighbouring countries benefit from new insights. To avoid lagging behind these developments requires investment in geological and geophysical research. Also vitally important is a broader focus: not only known minerals such as gold, bauxite and oil should be sought, but also new potential mineral resources such as diamonds, manganese and rare earth elements.

The Geological Mining Service would have to play a leading role with regard to geological research, exploration for mineral deposits, supervising mining activities and attracting investors. But it has been unable to do this for years already, partly because of a lack of skilled personnel and equipment. There are long-standing plans to transform the Service into an up-to-date, autonomous organisation and empower it, both institutionally and materially, so that it can better supervise the mining sector, but those plans have not yet been realised.

Modern legislation is indispensable to attracting venture capital. The Surinamese mining law dates from 1986 and is regarded as obsolete, and the proposed replacement, which was drafted in 2004, has not yet become law. Modern legislation reduces or removes the discretionary powers of the Minister in charge of mining affairs, include regulations for protecting the social and physical environments, guarantees for investors, provisions for compensation procedures and rules for the preservation of minerals and public health.

To attract investors, a country should be competitive, stable, and have an established tax regime. In mining countries such as Canada, special tax and financing protocols have been developed that facilitate the financing of mining projects. Private investors who buy shares in prospecting companies and thus underwrite the risk, can deduct the purchase from their income tax returns. To attract venture capital for initial exploration and exploitation Suriname will have to adopt a highly progressive, competitive and transparent policy

Whenever the development of the mining sector is discussed the environmental aspect cannot be disregarded. International environmental organisations have successfully resisted large-scale mining projects in India, Guatemala and Indonesia because of the resulting destruction of the physical environment. In addition, the effect of large-scale projects on the social environment is important. The gold mining projects in neighbouring Guyana and Venezuela have provoked some serious problems among local populations.

Mining engineer Manuel Gonzaga de Souza tests the gold-bearing material in the pit, Benzdorp, 2007.
Photo: Marjo de Theije

Mining now and in the future

In addition to the mature bauxite, gold and oil industries, Suriname also has a few others such as kaolin and natural stone quarrying that are showing growth. The following overview discusses the current state of affairs in each sector with particular attention given to new industries.

Bauxite

In June 2014 Suralco's parent company Alcoa advised the Suriname government that they would only continue operating in the bauxite and alumina industry in Suriname under specific conditions. Since then, both parties have been in discussions to try and resolve Suralco's concerns about the long-term prospects and the problems with energy supply. Time will reveal the outcome of these negotiations and whether the bauxite industry in Suriname will survive. This step by Alcoa should probably be seen against the background of the company's decision to invest in processing aluminium into products and reduce the basic cost of the raw materials worldwide

It is clear that the importance of alumina to the Suriname's economy has decreased since the recent global economic recession. Between 2007 and 2012 alumina production reduced by almost half, which compelled Suralco to postpone all non-essential maintenance and freeze investments. Whether the bauxite reserves in West Suriname will still be exploited is also in doubt. This is likely to be expensive due to the relatively low alumina content in the ore (e.g., stocks in the Moengo and Coermotibo region and in the Commewijne and Onverdacht region show higher percentages), the cost of transporting the ore to Paranam (which will require dredging sections of the Corentyne River), and the necessity of adapting the alumina refinery in Paranam to make it suitable to process the ore from West Suriname.

Gold

Exports of gold in 2013 amounted to 62 per cent of Suriname's total exports. Small-scale mining in that year accounted for 67 per cent of the total production. This gold is from legal as well as illegal producers, with an estimated 25,000 workers. Formalisation of this sector is a government priority.

The potential gold reserves of the Guiana Shield, and thus also of Suriname, is very interesting for many exploration companies. New mines are developed from Venezuela to French Guyana. In Suriname we know of possible gold deposits in the Sarakreek region, Lely Mountains, the Selakreek, the Goliath-Tibiti region and Benzdorp. However, much will depend on the availability of energy. In this context, the implementation of the TapaJai Project that will increase electricity production from the hydroelectric power station by directing more water from the Tapanahony River to Afobaka Dam would be a favourable development.

Furthermore, as always the global gold price is an important factor. Due to the unfavourable gold price at the time of writing, Rosebel Gold Mines is being cautious when it comes to further investment and expanding its large-scale mining activities, which has a direct negative impact on state revenues. Now that the prices are so low, Surgold N.V., originally a joint venture between Newmont and Alcoa but now entirely in the hands of the former, is planning to develop a huge mine (total cost one billion US dollars) in the Nassau region in an effort to reduce operating costs worldwide. The small-scale gold mining industry is also experiencing a downturn because of lower gold prices.

According to analysts, among the reasons for the low price is the strengthening of the American dollar, weak global inflation, and the surplus of gold on the world market. The strong demand from China and the relaxation of import duties in India have had a positive influence on the price. Geopolitical developments can also affect the price. If the price remains low, it has a braking effect on exploration activities and further developments in the gold industry. Under such conditions, large companies will ask the government for additional amenities.

Petroleum

In Suriname the petroleum industry takes second place after gold mining in terms of export value. In 2013 petroleum and petroleum products exports were worth 512 million USD. It is expected that production will increase. State Oil wants to transform itself into a broader energy company, which handles the production and distribution of petroleum and petroleum products, ethanol and thermal electricity. Plans exist for the construction of an ethanol plant in Wageningen that will produce 40 million litres annually. The search for oil reserves and seismic surveys also continue in Suriname's territorial waters, but commercially viable quantities of petroleum have yet to be found. Nevertheless, expectations are positive. State Oil's partner, Tullow Oil, has tapped oil in Ghana and French Guyana (still not commercially viable in French Guyana, however), and the knowledge and insights gained in those countries increases the likelihood of success in Suriname.

As other minerals the oil industry is also exposed to fluctuations in the price of the raw material. Lower world prices reduced State Oil's sales and profits for 2013. The expectation is that in the medium term oil prices will not fall below the 2013 level and that the petroleum industry will therefore continue to play an important role in Suriname's economy for years to come. Bringing production in the country's territorial waters online would certainly boost the economy.

Building materials

From the literature it is known that there is a connection between gross domestic product (GDP) and the use of building materials. An increase in one increases the other. There was an enormous growth in the production of building materials between 2010 and 2012, followed by a sharp decline in 2013 (see Table 2). Suriname's GDP rose from 4.2 per cent in 2010 to 5.3 per cent in 2011, then dropped in 2012 to 3.9 per cent,

SCPS Power Plant.
Photo: State Oil

before rising again to 4.4 per cent in 2013. In 2012 producers of building materials apparently did not foresee the decline in demand for their products, and they therefore responded strongly in 2013 to the decline of 2012. The reality was that this was just as an expansion of the economy became apparent. Demand for and the production of building materials will therefore always lag behind GDP.

Kaolin

Kaolin (also known as China clay or *pembadoti*) is a white clay consisting mainly of the mineral kaolinite, which already has quite a long history in Suriname. The inland peoples in particular have a long tradition of mining and washing kaolin for use in their cultural and social activities.

Kaolin belongs to the group of industrial minerals. Some industrial minerals are well-defined products that are marketed according to standard specifications. However, many others, including kaolin, are produced for a variety of specific purposes and therefore appear in varying qualities depending on the application. Having sufficient knowledge about these varying applications is vital.

Since 1949, the government and international companies operating in Suriname have conducted research into the presence and applications of kaolin. These research activities have not resulted in the development and exploitation of kaolin deposits. Kaolin occurs in various places in Suriname, and not necessarily with bauxite. The most extensive deposits are found in east Suriname, for example, in the vicinity of Moengo, where they are below the bauxite layer. Surveys of this area, which is the best assayed to date, indicate the presence of more than 60 million tons of kaolin of reasonable to good quality. Kaolin also occurs in the Onverdacht region, the Bakhuis region in West Suriname, along the road to Afobaka, along the Brownsweg near Pokigron, and possibly at Rama and Jorkakreek.

The main industrial applications of kaolin are in the paper and ceramics industries. It is also used in the pharmaceutical, cosmetic, and paint industries and in the manufacture of plastics and rubber. The paper pigment market for the Surinamese kaolin is the most lucrative, which is why most studies and exploitation efforts have focused on this market. The Surinamese company Moengo Minerals ultimately came the closest to actually producing and exporting high-quality pigments for the paper industry. In 2002 it began its exploration activities in the Moengo region, but partly because of the global economic crisis and the decline in international demand for kaolin for paper pigments, the planned construction of a kaolin pigment factory has not yet begun. As an alternative, Moengo Minerals has developed metakaolin, a processed clay that can be added to cement to create more durable concrete and which in part can also be used as a replacement for cement.

Large quantities of kaolin are also used in the ceramic and cosmetic industries. In the early 1990s the State-owned company Para Industries used kaolin as a raw material for its ceramics, but this company existed only briefly. Some small-scale ceramic producers

Mining kaolin in the Moengo.
Photo: Moengo Minerals

still use it. Only one producer in the cosmetic industry uses kaolin in its products. Currently Moengo Minerals has the most kaolin expertise. The further development of our kaolin reserves requires closer cooperation between Moengo Minerals and other private companies, which together should assay the reserves and the applications of kaolin and determine the types of investment required to further this industry. Other issues to be examined include to what extent the creation of an export-oriented ceramic industry is feasible, how metakaolin can be used on a wide scale in construction and infrastructure development, how the export of metakaolin can be promoted, and what other kaolin applications and products can be developed and/or produced, whether or not in cooperation with foreign partners.

Natural stone

Natural stone is a generic term for various types of rocks – for example, marble, granite, basalt, gneiss and dolerite – which are mined and processed according to certain dimensions or specifications for construction. Already in the eighteenth century natural stone was quarried at Worsteling Jacob along the Suriname River for the

Metakaolin storage.
Photo: Moengo Minerals

construction of parts of Fort Zeelandia, marking the beginning of the natural stone industry in Suriname.

Products from the natural stone industry can be broadly divided into semi-bulk and specialty products. Semi-bulk products are various kinds of building blocks made from natural stone. Besides physical and chemical properties, the colour and the texture of the rock also determine its future use.

Specialist stone products include tiles, countertops, tombstones and panels. Almost all these products are made of large stone blocks with a volume of about seven cubic metres and a weight of 20 tons, which are mined in a quarry. Transporting these blocks makes heavy demands on the infrastructure: roads and bridges must be built to carry the weight. In 1985, the privately owned company, N.V. Graniet, began quarrying rocks in West Suriname and processing them into tiles, monuments and countertops for the local market and for export. Nowadays, the company works with imported granite slabs.

Natural stone destined for decorative purposes is often used in projects that may take years to complete. It is thus of vital importance for an architect or developer that the required amount of the agreed quality of rock can be delivered for the duration of the project. Essential for this market therefore is the reliability of the suppliers and guaranteed prices. A new natural stone manufacturer therefore has the greatest chance of success if he works on his marketing and sales with a company that has already built up a trustworthy reputation in the industry.

In view of Suriname's geology the development of a diversified, export-focused natural stone industry hold promise. In the ten years from 1980 to 1990, the government, in collaboration with the United Nations Industrial Development Organization (UNIDO) and the United Nations Development Programme (UNDP), initiated a study of the potential of industrial minerals, including natural stone. The Geological Mining Service and Consulting Services N.V. identified various locations with (relatively) easily accessibility and recoverable deposits during that period.

The recoverability of the various deposits has not yet been properly investigated. Intensive exploration and mining surveys are necessary before it can be concluded for which type of product a deposit is appropriate. The only location where such research has been done is at Kale Rots near Patamacca, a massive rock formation along the road to Langatabbetje, about 30 kilometres south of Moengo. Natural stone blocks were excavated in Patamacca in the 1990s, and more recently as well; most of these were exported.

Several specific conditions for each market type will have to be met to continue developing Suriname's natural stone industry. As with many sectors, the local market is limited and the greatest problem facing this progress is the lack of a good sector-specific infrastructure. Some support and guidance from the government is therefore essential. Besides general production-enhancing measures, such as tax incentives, facilitating export procedures and constructing and maintaining a suitable physical infrastructure, good cooperation between the government and the private sector is crucial.

The potential of other minerals

The Geological Mining Service has investigated the presence in Suriname of minerals such as manganese, diamonds, chromium, copper and iron. The results were not encouraging, but they may have been affected by the techniques used at the time. Modern insights into the geological evolution of the Guiana Shield make it prudent to search again for diamonds, manganese, chromium, tin, phosphate, silica sands and rare earth elements. This will allow for more accuracy regarding the occurrence of these minerals and the economic viability of extracting them.

Diamonds
Diamonds were first discovered in Suriname in the Suriname River in the vicinity of Berg en Dal in 1880. Over time, diamonds have mainly been found in the Rosebel Formation in the Rosebel region near Brokopondo. Surveying for diamonds has also occurred at other locations along the Suriname River and in the savannah region in the vicinity of Zanderij and Tafelberg. Until the 1980s, the Geological Mining Service investigated the origin of the diamonds, but was unable to establish it. In 2012, the Canadian exploration company Canasur Gold Ltd. conducted exploration activities in the Goliath-Tibiti region. Indications are that diamond-bearing kimberlite pipes could be located there.

Manganese, chromium, tin

A survey by the Geological Mining Service between 1953 and 1960 revealed that manganese occurs in several places in Suriname, including in the vicinity of the Sarakreek along the Suriname River, along the Tapanahony River and around Apoema Soela on the left bank of the Marowijne River. However, the survey at that time showed no economically viable deposits.

During the period 1966 to 1975 small chromium deposits were found in the surroundings of the Emma mountain range, Tukumutukreek area along the Saramacca River and in an area west of the Upper Saramacca River. Tin deposits have been recorded in northeast Suriname, as well as in the Jorkakreek area along the Marowijne River, and in the Rama area along the Suriname River.

Rare earth elements

Rare earth elements such as neodymium, cerium, scandium, and yttrium are typically not found concentrated in economically exploitable ore deposits. These elements have a variety of applications such as in alloys, in the automotive industry, in electronics and in laser and communications technologies. The Geological Mining Service found indications of these elements in the 1960s in the Bakhuis region in West Suriname. The mineral monazite – one of the main sources of rare earth elements – occurs in several locations: in placer deposits (an accumulation of minerals formed by gravity separation during sedimentary processes), rivers, creeks, and weathered and metamorphosed rocks.

Phosphate and silica sand

The surveys conducted by the Geological Mining Service during the 1960s in West Suriname also detected phosphate reserves throughout the Bakhuis region. Silica or white quartz sands occur primarily in Suriname's savannah, the so-called Zanderij landscape, but also in the vicinity of Jodensavanne and the Bakhuis Mountains. Results have shown that after processing, these sands would be suitable for the glass industry. N.V. Glasinsur in Suriname actually used these sands in the 1990s for exactly this purpose.

Suriname: a mining country?

In 1995 the World Bank ranked Suriname as the world's seventeenth richest country in terms of availability of natural resources. Minerals play an important role in this wealth because of their strategic significance and their impact on other sectors of the economy. They are also appealing because investors can accrue large profits from them and countries can enjoy the benefits: income, employment and development.

However, the acquisition of wealth from minerals is dependent on the extent to which Suriname as a nation is able to find and exploit them. Regardless of how agreeable our geological circumstances may appear, in comparison with, for example, Brazil,

Chile, Peru and Ghana, the size of our territory will probably only yield a limited return. Moreover, in themselves favourable geological conditions for the exploitation of a mineral deposit are not enough: a positive market situation that appeals to venture capital is required, as is proficient management, sufficient expertise, and a government commitment to research and exploration.

Iamgold plant.
Collection Iamgold

Finally, we must realise that developing countries with substantial mineral resources often have relatively poor economic growth figures, and that these resources are finite. Thus, the mining sector does not have a sustainable character. It is essential that the revenue from this sector partly be used to further developing sectors that are sustainable.

Literature

British Geological Survey, 'Creating a Minerals Institute in Suriname – Preparatory Study', 1989.

Central Bank of Suriname: Various publications.

Chender, M., *Global Exploration Trends*. Metals Economics Group: CESCO International Exploration Forum, 2013.

Dahlberg, E.H., 'Delfstofvoorkomens en mijnbouwbeleid in Suriname', Geological and Mining Service (GMD), Internal Report, 1984.

Dardenne M.A. & Schobbenhaus C., 'Metallogeny of the Guiana Shield', in: *Géologie de la France*, no. 2-3-4 (2003) pp. 291–319.

Ferrier, D.J.H. (ed.), *Gedenkboek van het ministerie van Natuurlijke Hulpbronnen: 1958-2008 vijftig jaar ministerie van Natuurlijke Hulpbronnen*. Paramaribo: Centrum voor Economisch en Sociaal Wetenschappelijk Onderzoek, CESWO, 2010.

Gemerts, G.M., 'Paper to be Presented at the Technical Workshop Exploitation, Extraction and Upgrading of Industrial Minerals, UNIDO-Czechoslovakia Joint Programme, Non-Metallic Industries, Pilsen'. Geological and Mining Service (GMD) of Suriname, 1992.

Gemerts, G.M., 'Some Notes on the Occurrence of Natural Stones in Suriname'. Geological and Mining Service (GMD) of Suriname, 1993. (Internal report)

Geological and Mining Service (GMD) of Suriname, 'De recente ontwikkelingen m.b.t. andere delfstoffen dan bauxiet en de toekomstperspectieven, Seminar', in: *Stadszending Paramaribo* (1988).

Hakstege, A.L., 'Exploration and Exploitation of Industrial Minerals in Suriname', in: Th. E. Wong et al. (eds.), *The History of Earth Sciences in Suriname*, p. 367–75. Amsterdam: Royal Netherlands Academy of Arts and Sciences, 1998.

Hill, L., 'Newmont Plans $1 Billion Suriname Gold Mine to Cut Costs' (Accessed via: http://www.bloomberg.com/news/2014-07-29/newmont-approves-construction-of-suriname-gold-mine.html, accessed 9 August 2014).

International Council on Mining & Metals, 'Trends in the Mining and Metals Industry. Mining's Contribution to Sustainable Development'. London: ICMM, 2012. (Accessed via: http://www.icmm.com/document/4441)

Krook, L., 'Sediment Petrographical Studies in Northern Suriname', in: *Contributions to the Geology of Suriname*, vol. 9, Geological and Mining Service (GMD) of Suriname, 1984.

Lie A Kwie, C.J., Esajas, H.G. & Parisius, A.J.J., *80 jaar bauxietindustrie in Suriname*. Paramaribo: Suralco L.L.C., 1996.

Ontwikkelingsplan 2012-2016, Suriname in transformatie. The Government of Suriname, February 2012.

Rambaran Mishre, A.D., 'Diamant en haar voorkomen in Suriname'. Paramaribo: Anton de Kom University of Suriname, 1986. (Seminar report)

State Oil Company Suriname N.V., 'Staatsolie behoudt status "Billion Dollar Company"'. State Oil press release, 28 March 2014.

Suralco Magazine, vol. 9, no. 3 (1977).

'Suriname in de ban van goud', *Kompas Weekblad*, vol. 1, no. 271 (1986).

'Technical Report Goliat (Tibiti) Project, Sipaliwini District Eastern Suriname'. CanaSur Gold Ltd, 2012.

United States Geological Survey, *Minerals Yearbook, French Guiana, Guyana and Suriname* (Advance release), 2011.

Vletter, D.R. de, 'Economic Geology and Mineral Potential of Suriname', in: *Contributions to the Geology of Suriname*, vol. 8, pp. 91–129. Geological and Mining Service (GMD) of Suriname, 1984.

Vletter, D.R. de, 'The Quest for Diamonds in Suriname', in: Th. E Wong et al. (eds.), *The History of Earth Sciences in Suriname*, p. 351-65. Amsterdam: Royal Netherlands Academy of Arts and Sciences, 1998.

For many years geologist **Glenn Gemerts** was head of Suriname's Geological Mining Service (GMD) and vice president of Mining for the Ministry of Natural Resources. He was president and CEO of the State mining corporation, NV Grassalco, for a number of years and is now a consultant to the company.

No time to lose

The importance of education to Suriname's development

Marie Levens

Nowadays, every country can develop a good schooling system that is rooted in the true meaning of the word 'education', from the Latin *educere*, which means 'to lead', 'to take care of', or 'to grow'. In Suriname, the improvement of the education system stems from the collective intelligence, the diversity, and the fortitude of our people. We are aware that without accessible education for everyone it is impossible to eradicate poverty and reduce child mortality, or stimulate economic growth and bring about social integration. To this end, the Surinamese government has paid special attention to teachers training, built schools across the country, and took it upon itself to develop a curriculum oriented towards the country's own context many years ago. While the discussion about the future of our education system is still ongoing, we can accomplish a great deal to bring about universal and high-quality education.

We are living in an age of opportunity when it comes to economic development. Regional banks have taken more responsibility for local problems, reducing regional countries' dependence on international banks. The government is implementing specific policies to enhance resistance to the whims of global markets, expand trade relations, improve Internet access, and better distribute development opportunities among the population in the districts and the interior of the country. Suriname has managed to tackle several deeply rooted problems. However, we must not forget that global economic development is inextricably bound up with local socio-economic development, giving rise to new issues that require new policies and solutions. Economic growth and educational development go hand in hand.

Opportunities for growth are directly proportional to the opportunities to learn and produce new knowledge. Suriname can no longer simply rely on its natural resources and mining industry if it wants to keep developing. The country has to focus on an as yet unused *national* resource: our teachers.

Pupils at primary schools in the interior of Suriname often travel long distances to attend their lessons. Photo: Toon Fey

A school teacher in the classroom with students. Photo: Toon Fey

Teachers have always been multipliers. When they receive high-quality professional support, they are capable of developing and accelerating new ways of thinking, new knowledge, and new abilities. In so doing, teachers push the economy forward with tangible results. Moreover, they can do this in a short period of time, and at a fraction of the cost of traditional approaches to investment and production. Both in Paramaribo and the interior, properly trained and engaged teachers can expand our national capacity by teaching students how to think in innovative, critical, inquiring, analytical, and problem-solving ways. Technology and the sciences can help students develop their capacities in that direction, so that we will no longer have to look abroad for solutions to the problems we are experiencing now (or expect in the future).

Training professional teachers to be sufficiently equipped for the 21st century calls for a scientific approach rather than an intuitive one. Professional teacher training is necessary in every phase of the educational life cycle. We have to seriously investigate how we can make that happen in an enduring way: how we can guide them, support individual educational possibilities, permanently and sustainably strengthen educational institutes, and contribute to the critical balance between economic growth and general development. This chapter discusses Suriname's potential, its teachers, and its children, and concludes with specific recommendations.

Surinamese Pedagogical Institute (SPI), where primary education (kindergarten and primary school) teachers are trained.
Photo: Ingrid Moesan

The complex balance between growth, equality, and education

Banks, academics, politicians, development organisations, the private sector, and educational institutes worldwide agree on the principles of education and integrated development. As Nicholas Kristof of *The New York Times* writes, 'Vaccines save lives. Iodizing salt raises I.Q.s and reduces mental disability. Wells, bed nets and deworming improve health. Family planning would help the 215 million women worldwide who yearn for a way to avoid getting pregnant. Education allows people to transform their own lives.'

Education has always been the binding factor in general development. Better education is linked to greater equality, growth in GDP, improved general health, and more civic participation. Conversely, an outdated education system, inattention to students' needs, a lack of educational tools, and irrelevant teacher training can be linked to deteriorating general health, more inequality, vulnerability to natural disasters, civic indifference, and an increased likelihood that young people will feel attracted to (or become victims of) crime and violence. An extra year of education makes for a 10 per cent increase in an individual's income. Education improves children's health: a child whose mother can read has 50 per cent more chance of living longer than five years. The return on investment is high. This is why, traditionally, education in Suriname is virtually free. Moreover, school children in this country have been receiving free meals for a few years now, and there are after-school programmes with homework tuition and sports activities. According to the Economic Commission for Latin America and the Caribbean (ECLAC), inequality in Latin America and the Caribbean has declined significantly in several sectors over the past twenty years, as has poverty.

The problems and consequences of unbalanced development

However, investments to strengthen the education system have not kept pace with, or are concealed behind, the rising emphasis on growth. Several Latin America and Caribbean countries are paying the price for this. Since 2012, optimism about new markets opportunities has slowly waned. Both the government's and the country's

The Ministry of Education and Community Development (Minov) introduces ICT to the education system during Global Money Week in March 2014. Photo: Sven Tjon-A-Meeuw. Collection Minov

foreign debts have risen. In Suriname, mergers between mining companies have put pressure on profits. Faith in the durability of high growth rates has declined throughout the area. In some regions, this situation has seen the return of old fears about macro-economic and financial crises.

ECLAC reports that in 2012, 28.2 per cent of the population in Latin America and the Caribbean lived in poverty, of which 11.3 per cent were in extreme poverty or destitute circumstances. In absolute numbers, this means that 164 million people were poor, of which 66 million were extremely poor. The story becomes even more harrowing when we realise that in today's global economy, information is the main medium of exchange. According to the World Economic Forum, the big gap between the field of knowledge and innovative capacity in Latin America has hindered our potential. There are too few prospects for upward mobility, which is why people seek higher education and better economic opportunities outside the region. On its own, the current redistribution policy cannot compensate for the lack of education.

The Surinamese people recognise the power of education as a gateway to new opportunities, welfare, and economic growth. The United Nations Development Programme's (UNDP) Human Development Atlas for Suriname 2013 convincingly shows that people are very aware of the issues our country has to solve. Respondents were asked to name the three most pressing problems from a list of fourteen: education ranked third, directly after housing and employment.

What does Suriname's future look like from the viewpoint of several international organisations? A 2014 report by the World Bank states that poverty and inequality levels remain causes for concern. In 2012, the country ranked 105 out of 187 on the UNDP's Human Development Index. The Food and Agriculture Organization (FAO) estimates that 15 to 20 per cent of the population is malnourished. Moreover, there are major differences between the coastal areas, which usually are wealthier, and the inland.

The UNDP Environment and Energy Group also recently reported that Suriname lacks both the human and the financial capacity to fully benefit from its development potential. In 2013, the governor of the Central Bank of Suriname articulated the problem: a rigid and antiquated public sector.

The high cost of low-quality education

A consistent pattern is unfolding in Latin America and the Caribbean: more schools, newer textbooks, and an effective enrolment policy are necessary, but no longer sufficient, education system reforms. Schools with unqualified teaching staff lead to more inequality, and unsafe neighbourhoods and school buildings make studying impossible. The UNDP points out that more enrolment in all layers of the education system should go hand in hand with programmes that ensure fewer repeaters, more graduates, and overall improvement of the quality of education. Proper schooling stimulates economic growth, innovation, social equality, and cohesion, both directly and indirectly. The education sector should be shielded from economic cutbacks.

The issue of repeating students is a larger problem than it may seem at first. Governments in the region spend over 12 million US dollars on this per year because they are paying for the costs of extra classrooms and more teachers. In Latin America the costs even mount to 19.9 million US dollars, three times the amount calculated for primary and higher education trajectories worldwide. UNESCO states that repeating the first classes is strongly linked to problems with transmitting reading and writing skills. Research points to significant obstacles: antiquated pedagogical methods and an outmoded understanding of language and children's learning processes. The situation worsens in a bilingual or multilingual context in which students (and often teachers as well) have to study (and teach, respectively) in an unfamiliar language. Repeating is a problem in Suriname, where it also obstructs development. Attempts have been made to keep the construction costs of schools within limits by assembling classes combining children from different age groups, but if lessons in those classes are not differentiated, older students will still turn their backs on schooling.

A starting point for better quality

Education reforms begin at home. The family plays a vital role in the development of children's cognitive capacities and other characteristics from birth. If that process goes well, the likelihood that they will apply their abilities to improve themselves is significantly enhanced. Disadvantaged children, especially those whose parents have a low socio-economic status, have far fewer chances to develop these types of essential abilities before their compulsory education begins at primary school. As a consequence, a large number of young people leave the education system without the knowledge and skills needed to do even the lowest-paying jobs.

When families receive help with these issues, it increases their children's chances of developing into engaged students and strengthens their resilience to any negative influences and other obstacles on their way to higher education. The school system therefore has to be founded on a relevant and robust primary school system in which the family plays an important role as well.

As we roll out our new national curriculum for Suriname, we must support teachers who are able to couple knowledge to the skills students need to fully develop in the 21st century: working together, thinking critically and in a problem-solving way, and conducting enquiry-based research in all subjects – with a special focus on the sciences and modern technology. Portfolios and ongoing assessments have proven to be much more effective than incoherent, written tests. New skills for our future require new teaching abilities as well as guidelines drawn up specifically for primary and secondary education.

Institute of Graduate Studies and Research (IGSR) of the Anton de Kom University of Suriname (Adekus). Higher education in Suriname faces numerous challenges, the greatest of which concerns the education and training of qualified and effective senior management.
Photo: Ingrid Moesan

Higher education should be seen as a national laboratory for innovative research, and as integral to development and the struggle against poverty. Suriname's rich biodiversity could be an endless source of research and the development of groundbreaking solutions to global problems, but for that to happen, the country has to formulate policies regarding its research priorities. At the moment, for example, more students are studying for a degree in social sciences at the Anton de Kom University than in the physical, technological, and biological sciences.

To develop such policies, we need to collect up-to-date and reliable data about Suriname's population, analyse and distribute it, and increase cooperation and coordination between different policy sectors. With useful data and information systems, our data-driven policy choices can identify shortcomings in legislation and policy, determine which applications are best, and choose appropriate strategies and programmes.

Suriname has made significant strides to address the challenge with regards to higher education by building connections with universities in the region and around the world. In doing so, the country increases its own strength when it comes to institutional abilities and the professionalisation of administration, management, infrastructure, and research programmes. We need to develop new disciplines for teachers that emphasise

A discussion between a teacher and a group of students. Photo: Sven Tjon-A-Meeuw. Collection Minov

ICT and the integral approach of the sciences by means of exact science and modern techniques. We also need support for teachers, curriculum developers, inspectors, school directors and civil servants working on integrating Suriname's new policy towards to ICT and science. Suriname wants to change, and is working hard to do so.

Problems and opportunities for teacher training

It is imperative that the new training programmes for teachers, based on research, science, and technology succeed. Expectations are high, but there are many concerns too. Teacher development programmes in the region often emphasise general, theoretical concepts instead of practical needs and everyday issues. For instance, future teachers do not learn how to deal with vulnerable, socially disadvantaged, and disabled children. There is a lack of attention to cooperation in the classroom, teacher collaboration, and individually tailored lessons, despite growing evidence that these competences characterise schools that perform well. Twenty-first century teaching and learning have often not been implemented in teacher training. Simply put, most teachers still work the way they did before. This means our youth are being prepared for the past rather than for now and the future.

Moreover, circumstances do not encourage highly qualified and talented students to become teachers. There are few incentives to build up good skills in their specific area of study and transfer that knowledge to children in remote districts and the interior. There is little encouragement to become professional mentors of education and development. However, Suriname has begun to take significant steps in that direction, which is promising.

In society, education as a profession is often seen in a negative light. For instance, it is thought that someone becomes a teacher if she is not selected for a better degree; that the profession involves too much work; that the classrooms are overcrowded; and that being a teacher is undesirable because, if admitted to hospital, a teacher receives the lowest level of care. Nevertheless, teachers are seen as sources of hope for change. We must restore dignity to the teaching profession.

Conversations with teachers, after-school care providers, curriculum developers, school inspectors, school supervisors, and university personnel indicate that there is an impressive, yet unused, opportunity to learn with and from each other. Special practice groups for teachers offer a safe environment for asking questions, sharing practical examples, and problem solving.

Suriname recognises that ICT-driven education means more than having access to knowledge or a more efficient management of the lessons. The use of ICT shifts a teacher's focus as being the only source of knowledge to being a facilitator who knows how to use the tools, and who can remove obstacles for students. ICT enhances teacher efficiency and effectiveness.

We do not have to wait for equipment to get started. Even without hardware, students can learn how to work with ICT. They can solve problems by sticking their written-down ideas to the wall with drawing pins, and then give shape to this information by moving these pieces of paper around, thereby increasing their collective knowledge. This is a good way to learn the basics of building a wiki or a blog. Students can prepare themselves for building websites by reading how to develop, present, and support an idea. Programmes that are aimed at the service sector can make use of existing community networks to simulate digital networks.

Radio stations and newspapers can teach media knowledge by discussing ideas that represent contrasting viewpoints. Computer games, puppet plays, learning by hearing and feeling and providing insights into complex ideas using local materials are just a few of several ways to prepare students and teachers for ICT in the education system, even if they do not own a computer.

Recommendations

Suriname cannot just emulate the strategies of larger, wealthier countries, or simply import solutions. The country's resilience and growth depend on our creativity, intellectual energy, and our ability to work together, think critically, and solve problems based on scientific research. Education is the catalyst of that change. Ideas stimulate growth, but growth does not always stimulate ideas. We need to find a balance between the two, and I hope my recommendations below go some way towards achieving this.

Teachers
- We have to renew the traditional teachers training model to attract more teachers with a passion for their profession and a true interest in children. They deserve new models that have already proven successful.
- Enable teachers to use their classrooms as laboratories where they can develop their own approaches to varying their classes.
- Stimulate collaboration and risk-taking. Where possible, enable teachers to use ICT and the Internet to build communities of practice. This stimulates a productive exchange of ideas between teachers in a safe environment, where experiences can be shared and problems solved. It provides room to think outside the box, and develop teaching applications tailored to local needs. Sharing knowledge, experiences, practical examples, risks and responsibilities makes us stronger.
- Encourage teachers to conduct their own research. Supplementary teacher training in this field can be integrated into the national curriculum. With research, they can nurture the students' curiosity; support locally relevant, innovative, and cooperative projects; organise scientific exhibitions, create social apprenticeships; mentor each other; and stimulate critical thinking and the ability to solve problems.
- Support the further development of tutoring programmes for recently graduated teachers, who should excel in three areas by demonstrating (1) a thorough command of professional knowledge, (2) teaching strategies that are creative and aimed at results, and (3) ongoing professional development and adult education.
- Give teachers time for additional training, and for observing each other's methods and strategies in the classroom.

School organisations
- Allow directors and school boards to adjust their schools' schedules, and to come up with their own, flexible solutions to issues regarding the students' work schedules and familial obligations.
- Allow room for curriculum developers and educators to work together directly with the teaching staff at school.
- Connect after-school care providers and classroom teachers, so that they can consult about individual students' performance and ways of learning.

The use of ICT in education will be increasingly important in the coming years. Students have to be taught the necessary skills as quickly as possible.
Private collection

- Diminish the dependence on textbooks for the transference of the national curriculum. They rapidly become out-of-date and should be complemented with other learning tools that can always be improved, adjusted, and mutually exchanged.
- Maintain and stimulate the fun of scientific research and thinking in the sciences, including exact sciences. Encourage science fairs, contests, and special exhibitions where children can solve problems. Such events can be underpinned with collaborations with the public and private sectors in Suriname, neighbouring countries, and the global scientific community.
- Couple the sciences (natural/social/humanitarian sciences, mathematics, chemistry) to the improvement of the community by focusing them on local needs and measurable effects. Not only can this contribute positively to issues that are important for the community, but it can also motivate students' and improve their performance.
- Consider new policies regarding teachers, and involve all parties in the process. Look at a teacher's training before and during their employment: the procedures for selection, hiring, promotion, evaluation, and discharge; teachers' criteria for demonstrating subject-matter mastery and teaching excellence; the content of teacher training programmes; expectations, wages and incentives.

General comments
- The significant increase in the number of hospital births and improved eating habits have been linked to effective pre-school programmes.
- A strong foundation with regard to language and maths stimulates children's higher cognitive skills and psychological resistance.
- Involving parents and families in schooling endorses learning in the classrooms, lowers medical costs, encourages healthy habits, increases school attendance, and diminishes the number of dropouts.
- Policies should be based upon this research.

A call to action

No country can instantly improve its entire school and teacher's training systems and deliver a generation of top-class innovators to bring about spectacular economic development. Measures can be taken, however, to make dramatic improvements to education quality and teacher professional development. Unfortunately, a lack of support for teachers perpetuates poor performance, undermining economic progress to an alarming degree. Because of the enormity of these problems, leaders have often been reluctant to take radical measures on behalf of teachers. They argue that education reform is far too costly, risky, and difficult to monitor and quantify. Others seek quick fixes by clinging to the unrealistic notion that ICT will solve development problems in no time. Strong teacher development programmes, supported by ICT, represent our most sustainable course.

That teachers are the driving force behind general development is indisputable. They interweave the historical and cultural memories of our country with attention for the current economic and social problems. Policymakers and leaders must clear the way so that teachers can reinvigorate their profession and transform teaching so that all children will want to be involved. They are the ones who can include families in their children's education, and who can intervene if school absenteeism occurs, thus helping to prevent the vicious circle that leads to a future without possibilities.

Our hope for integrated development in the 21st century rest on the shoulders of these teachers. The children of our country deserve the best possible education. The opportunities to take action are there. Now is the time.

Literature

ECLAC, 'Social Panorama of Latin America'. Economic Commission for Latin America and the Caribbean (ECLAC), 2013. (Accessed via: http://bit.ly/1rOkQjW)

Guzmán, J. et al., 'Effective Teacher Training Policies to Ensure Effective Schools. A Perspective from Central America and the Dominican Republic'. PREALblog, 2013. Accessed via: http://prealblog.files.wordpress.com/2013/12/teacher-policies-to-improve-ed-in-ca-english.pdf)

Gvirtz, S. & Torre, E., 'How Can We Build Good Educational Systems in Latin America?' *Education Week*, 18 October 2013. (Accessed via: http://blogs.edweek.org/edweek/international_perspectives/2013/10/how_can_we_build_good_educational_systems_in_latin_america.html)

Hoefdraad, G., 'Suriname Macroeconomic Outlook and Investment Opportunities. The 38th Annual Meeting of the Islamic Development Bank Group'. Dushanbe, 2013. (Accessed via: http://www.cbvs.sr/images/content/pdf/presentation-tajikistan-governor-hoefdraad-may2013-final.pdf)

Holm-Nielsen, L., Brunner, J., Balán, J., Thorn, K. & Elacqua, G., *Higher Education in Latin America and the Caribbean. Challenges and Prospects*. Santiago: UNESCO, 2004. (Accessed via: http://mt.educarchile.cl/archives/2005/08/higher_educatio.html)

Kristof, N., 'So Similar, So Different. For These Two Women, the Lottery of Birth Decides Opportunity'. *The New York Times*, 21 June 2014. (Accessed via: http://nyti.ms/1pURaTP)

Saavedra, J., 'Measuring Equality of Opportunity in Latin America. A New Agenda'. Banco Mundial, Poverty Reduction and Gender Group: Latin America and the Caribbean Region, 2009.

Sclafani, S., 'Asia Society. Recruiting, Training, and Supporting a 21st-Century Teaching Profession'. (Accessed via: http://asiasociety.org/education/learning-world/teacher-professional-development-international-practices)

UNDP REDD+ Team Readiness Preparation Proposal, 'Assessment note. On the Proposed Project with Suriname for REDD+ Readiness Preparation Support'. UNDP, 2013.

UNDP, 'Strengthening National Capacities of Suriname for the Elaboration of the National REDD+ Strategy and Design of its Implementation Framework'. Project Document UNDP.

UNDP, *Human Development Report. The Rise of the South. Human Progress in a Diverse World*. UNDP, 2013. (Accessed via: http://bit.ly/1lAWoOL)

UNDP, *The Global Conversation Begins. Emerging Views for a New Development Agenda*. UNDP, 2013.

UNICEF, *Global Initiative on Out-Of-School Children. Finishing School. A Right for Children's Development. A Joint Effort*. Executive Summary, Latin America and the Caribbean. UNICEF, 2012.

United Nations Suriname, *The United Nations Development Assistant Framework 2012-2016 for Suriname*. UN Suriname, 2012. (Accessed via: http://sr.one.un.org/united-nations-development-assistance-framework-2012-2016-action-plan)

UNDP, *Human Development Atlas for Suriname*. UNDP, 2013. (Accessed via: http://undpsuriname.org)

Vaillant, D., 'IBE Preparing Teachers for Inclusive Education in Latin America'. UNESCO, 2011.

World Bank, *Suriname Overview*. World Bank, 2014. (Accessed via: http://www.worldbank.org/en/country/suriname/overview#1)

World Economic Forum, *The Global Competitiveness Report. Latin America and the Caribbean*. World Economic Forum, 2014. (Accessed via: http://reports.weforum.org/the-global-competitiveness-report-2013-2014)

Marie Levens is the former Minister of Foreign affairs of Suriname (2000–5). She received an advanced degree in Educational Sciences in the Netherlands after receiving a teaching degree in her own country. She has been involved in education in Suriname for many years, including as head of the Bureau Education and Study Facilities (BOS) of the Ministry of Education and Community Development. As the director of the Department of Human Development, Education and Employment she currently manages and is responsible for innovation in education and capacity strengthening in the OAS member states.

Deeply rooted in society

De Surinaamsche Bank and corporate social responsibility

Chandra van Binnendijk

De Surinaamsche Bank N.V. (DSB) is deeply rooted in Surinamese society, and it is determined to invest this fact with content and meaning. In the 21st century, it is more obvious than ever that a healthy business goes hand in hand with a close engagement with society. The bank has formulated its commitment as three primary corporate principles: economic performance, respect for the social aspects of life, and respect for the environment. Together these three principles form the basis of DSB's attitude towards doing business, an approach that in business is called 'socially responsible'.

From these three guiding principles, the bank has developed core values that all departments refer to as a guide in how to interact with customers. This set of values and standards includes procedures on what to do if an employee suspects criminal activity and money laundering, a scheme for whistleblowers, guidelines relating to the use of information, and ethical rules for dealing with gifts and securities transactions. All 400 of the bank's employees are rigorously trained in these core values.

DSB explains in its long-range plan how it views its social responsibility and how it intends to provide it with content. This chapter provides an overview of the ways in which the bank will realise these objectives in practice.

Financing

For DSB corporate social responsibility means, firstly, looking carefully at the types of businesses DSB facilitates when issuing loans. DSB director Sigmund Proeve is particularly clear and direct about these considerations: 'If you finance everything and everyone who asks for it, you are in fact only a moneylender. Sometimes you might be financing something good, but which is socially undesirable. For example, we know that mercury contributes to environmental pollution, so we will not finance a mercury

DSB's headquarters.
Collection DSB

importer, even if he has a license. Casinos are not among our customers, because we want no part in gambling addiction. We refused to open bank accounts for a few hundred girls as was recently asked of us, because they were found to be providing a webcam sex service. In such cases, you no longer prioritise your business, but the society. That's what you should serve as a company. We are after all one small molecule in that society.'

Nature

One of the strategic objectives of the long-range plan is to promote conservation and the sustainable exploitation of Suriname's natural resources. That means, first, that we must explicitly take into account environmental issues such as green energy, waste separation, reduced paper consumption and careful sourcing of materials when constructing and using our own bank branches. DSB is currently investigating the possibilities of using solar energy for its bank buildings in the near future. Furthermore, responsible waste disposal measures are being taken at all our offices. Where once all the waste ended up in one dustbin, we now separate and process our refuse in a responsible way. The bank also has an agreement with a customer who recycles waste paper – DSB shreds the paperwork, the customer picks it up and recycles it into paper towels and toilet paper. So it isn't always about large and dazzling actions, but small actions that make a contribution too.

DSB is also partnered with the conservation organisation Suriname Conservation Foundation (SCF). Along with thirteen other companies, the bank empowers this collective in its management and conservation of biodiversity in our country. Soon the partners will make a joint financial contribution to support SCF projects that emphasises the preservation of Suriname's biodiversity. The bank sends an unambiguous signal with all these activities: it wants to set a high standard, because that is what contributes to a better society.

Society

The extent to which DSB gives something back to society is additional evidence of its social commitment. For this, a sponsorship policy has been formulated that enables focused choices for specific target groups and sectors. Several institutions that are committed to sports, arts and culture, education and the environment, receive financial support based on this. However, the applicants are expected to make a contribution too. They submit a sponsorship application to DSB, where a commission decides which ones can be honoured according to the criteria of the policy. Building

DSB director Sigmund Proeve (left) with SCF chairman Nardi Johanns (middle). With the Suriname Conservation Foundation, the Bank is an active participant in the green partnership for conservation.
Collection DSB

maintenance is usually excluded from sponsorship, as it touches on a point of contention with the government: DSB pays its taxes, and feels that it is the duty of the State to maintain public buildings from that income.

Institutions that can rely on regular financial assistance from the bank include organisations for socially disadvantaged and the elderly, as well as the Children's Book Festival Foundation – DSB director Sigmund Proeve is even president of this foundation. Through this foundation DSB contributes to various activities that promote good reading habits in young people such as reading campaigns, the national championship reading evening, and organising the festival in various districts.

Another example is the social tradition of the DSB Christmas concert. Each year, more than 6000 visitors come and enjoy the music. The bank invites children and the elderly from different care homes each year as special guests. Easily 80 DSB employees happily volunteer for the month of December to make this event a pleasant reality.

DSB director Proeve involves himself closely with promoting the pleasure of reading among school pupils.
Collection DSB

The banking sector

Within the bankers association, of which all nine commercial banks in Suriname are members, the companies fine-tune issues relating to monetary and business economics with each other. Corporate social responsibility is a regular item on the agenda as an

It wouldn't really be Christmas without DSB's Christmas concert! Thousands of people look forward to this festive period at the end of each year. Choirs and musicians fill the air with their sweetest sounds.
Collection DSB

issue that concerns the entire banking sector. In matters such as debit card fraud, the banks jointly campaign to make everyone aware of it. Even the banks that were unaffected by it participate. Such cooperation does not imply that there is collusion in the banking sector – which would imply that it was operating as a cartel, a detrimental phenomenon. Moreover, DSB is pleased with the distinction between the companies, as it allows each bank to profile itself as it sees fit.

Alert and engaged

The way in which DSB gives substance to the notion of social entrepreneurship in the 21st century is mainly characterised by two aspects: engagement and a critical attitude. As far as the bank is concerned both aspects go hand in hand and are not mutually exclusive; in the fact the bank holds the opposite to be true. Engagement manifests itself precisely by being actively involved in what is happening in the society. For example, DSB's annual reports regularly analyse the government's Financial Accounts. When there was a shift in the allocation of state resources, for example, from social care to materiel, DSB sounded the alarm: it found spending less on citizens than on material things an unhealthy development.

DSB's board of directors regards being critical about government policy as one of its tasks; after all, it has a direct impact on the banking business and even more so on the national economy. Inflation, for example, or the unrestrained growth of the civil service are issues that require specific policies to rein them in. Being critical in a small society like Suriname is not without risks – criticism is not always popular, but DSB regards such vigilance as part of its commitment to corporate social responsibility.

DSB is not only alert and reactive to what happens beyond its walls and at the macro level: this approach is also applied internally. When applying for a loan, young employees are advised to avoid buying an expensive car, and put the money they save by settling for a cheaper one toward saving up for a house or a plot of land. In the beginning appreciation for such advice was in short supply. Yet gratitude for this positive interference by the employer has gradually increased and its usefulness is now widely acknowledged. Involvement brings with it a degree of interference, and DSB is proud to be engaged at this level.

Challenges and bottlenecks

With their call for socially responsible business practises, directors Sigmund Proeve and Henri Henar give meaning to a task that the bank set itself over a century ago: to not only function as a monetary mainstay, but also as a social one. This is not always easy, because each period has different challenges and bottlenecks that require tailored solutions. How do they deal with this? 'There is always an area of tension between your own motives as a bank and the government's policy. Also, the pace at which we work often differs from that of the government. Sometimes you even have to take a step or two backwards. But you have to keep going and stay on track. And you have to keep pestering them, you have to be bold and share your opinions with government ministers.'

In the process, they sometimes book small achievements that can be enormously motivating. 'For example, the establishment of the Institute for Natural Resources and Engineering Studies (NATIN) in Nickerie, after we had long pestered government ministers about the need for agricultural education in that district: the widespread urbanisation there is drawing people away from the land. We supported the Institute by providing computers. And initial positive results can already be seen: agriculture is once again becoming an activity that garners respect.' Despite this positive development, the two directors feel that still too little attention is paid to agricultural entrepreneurship. Ministers and other policy makers be forewarned – DSB will continue to bother you about national policy issues!

Tradition and modernity

Formulating new policies involves constantly striving for a workable balance between two factors that sometimes seem contradictory, but which are both important: preserving traditional values, and meeting the demands of modern life. Sometimes this challenge brings tough choices with it: something might be expedient on the one hand, technically speaking, but at the same time it could mean taking distance from respected traditions. After all, while encouraging innovation, DSB has always considered a certain consistency of paramount importance.

During the renovation of his office, bank director Mr Proeve faced such a dilemma head on. The energy inefficient windows in his office were in dire need of replacement, and the architect therefore advised removing the more than man-high glass panes. Yet Proeve said he would rather not replace them out of respect for architect Peter Nagel's design from the 1950s. Fortunately there was an excellent compromise solution that dealt with both aspects of the problem: a glass plate was placed in front of the beautiful high windows that saved enough energy so that the executive suite could get the 'environmentally friendly' seal of approval.

Giving off signals

It is certainly not the intention of DSB to pat themselves on the back and announce how well the bank is doing. 'If we remain as the only ones who draw attention to corporate social responsibility, then we have failed,' say Proeve and Henar. 'We do not want to stand alone; we want an increasing proportion of society to want to achieve these goals too. We do not pretend to have a solution, but we do give off signals.'

They therefore make their voices heard through the Suriname Conservation Foundation, for example, on issues such as mercury or other toxins in the environment. 'We support agriculture, so we don't ignore a customer who reports something like the misuse of pesticides. We offer guidance, for example, by making it possible for the farmer to be trained in better farming techniques. But because government policy places so little emphasis on agriculture, improvements in this area only happen very slowly.'

In contrast to agriculture, directors Proeve and Henar find that excessive time and attention is devoted to mining in Suriname. 'Of course we are not opposed to mining, it is a natural resource. But mining is finite, while agriculture is very durable. Bauxite once comprised more than 50 per cent of our exports, and now, 70 years later, we're wailing and gnashing our teeth because we've run out. Our children will have the same regrets in 50 years when the gold that everyone is focused on at the moment also runs out. It would be better to use the income from mining to develop the agricultural sector in a sustainable way. We support this kind of initiative.'

Microcredit and the importance of small businesses

Finally, corporate social responsibility is expressed in the union of the bank with the Microcredit Programme (MKP) that started four years ago. This connection runs through the Surinaamse Trust Maatschappij N.V., founded in 1952 as a subsidiary of DSB and better known by its abbreviated name Suritrust. Among its activities, Suritrust specialises in asset management for private and institutional investors. On behalf of the Ministry of Finance it currently acts as administrator of the funds that the State makes available to small business owners through the microcredit programme. Initially, the money for this came from Dutch relief funds, but after the Netherlands ceased the funding because of the Amnesty Law of 2012, the Surinamese government took over the programme and it has continued successfully. Within four years, the number of loans more than doubled and now thousands of small business owners have received assistance in the form of microcredit.

Loans from the Microcredit Programme are not granted immediately. Five organisations are involved as intermediaries: the credit cooperatives Godo and De Schakel, the Women's Business Group, the Seva Foundation in Nickerie, and Suritrust. These non-governmental organisations have the status of a microfinance institution (MFI) and in this capacity extend loans to their client base ranging from 100 Surinamese Dollars (SRD) to a maximum of 6000 SRD.

The volume of loans is probably modest in the world of banking, but this is about financial support that can change the fortunes of small business owners. For example, such a loan enables them to purchase a piece of equipment or a tool that allows them to preserve just a bit more fruit juice, to breed a few more sheep, or produce more black pudding, shaved ice or *pangis* (a type of cloth, also worn as a wrap). Often it all about that one extra impulse that can help a small business make a significant leap forward.

Office building of the Surinaamse Trust Maatschappij N.V., better known as Suritrust, where the microcredit programme for small businesses is managed on behalf of the Ministry of Finance. Collection DSB

The first evaluations

The first four-year cycle of the MKP ended in 2014. During that period, more than 4000 microloans were provided, including so-called repeat loans to approximately 2500 entrepreneurs. These businesses are part of a broad spectrum that embraces all sectors of the economy. Most of the loans went to the agricultural sector, with its numerous small-scale rice farmers, then to entrepreneurs engaged in handicraft production, and thirdly to the food industry.

The preliminary evaluations are favourable. With training and supervision from Suritrust, the five microfinance institutes (MFIs) mentioned above have increased their presence and added skills such as financial reporting and assessing applications. Micro-entrepreneurs, in turn, learned from the MFIs how to better manage their businesses and with a few exceptions, all parties fulfilled their obligations to the letter.

The Microcredit Programme is sure to continue and even be expanded. In the second half of 2014 Suritrust started a national campaign to involve more MFIs, to inform more micro-entrepreneurs about the programme, and to extend their activities from the coastal area to the hinterland, where the MKP is still little known, despite the inland being a hive of entrepreneurship and industriousness. The campaign has a catchy slogan: *Wan bigi okasi gi den pikin basi! ie!* ('A great opportunity for the little boss!').

DSB is committed to micro-entrepreneurs, who it regards as the backbone of society. At this bank they say: the chance of a thousand small business suddenly leaving your country is a thousand times smaller than the likelihood of one large company leaving. So it is entirely socially responsible to assist this special group of entrepreneurs, financially and otherwise.

Two micro-entrepreneurs

Jurgen Boodie and Abygail Jap-A-Joe

In 2009 Jurgen Boodie (35) and Abygail Jap-A-Joe (29) took a loan from Suritrust and opened JiJi's Restaurant. Assisted by family members, they worked hard to make it a success. After a few years they realised they could expand by taking over a neighbouring bar. In 2013, they applied for another loan – which they received – to pay the take-over costs, purchase furniture and fittings and increase the cold storage capacity. Actually they had really wanted a larger deep fryer, but their regular consultant at Suritrust advised them to wait a while before doing so. Creative as the couple are, they immediately came up with two appealing alternatives. Less frying? Then we'll serve more rice and pasta dishes. Serving customers with a modest income? Then we'll develop a special student menu – cheap but fun. After all, entrepreneurship is also recognising your weaknesses and working with what you have.

With the second loan Boodie and Jap-A-Joe's could expand JiJi's Restaurant from 26 to 48 seats. In 2013, the restaurant received a major regional award, the Citi Micro-Entrepreneurship Award for the Caribbean. This was a tremendous boost that came during a somewhat difficult period with hardly any customers and great anxiety about its survival. 'The award was a great encouragement to keep believing in what we do,' they said later. 'We are now in a more stable phase.' Dedicated personal commitment and a lot of financial sacrifices have been key to their success. Their revenue continues increasing, they now have nine employees, pay their bills promptly and in cash, and purchase nothing on account.

This entrepreneurial couple are brimful of ideas and would like to have more money to realise some of them, but they must match their enthusiasm to the possibilities. 'In the future we plan to expand or move to another location. We intend to focus on local customers rather than the tourists the restaurant now mainly attracts. Tourists are fine, but they're seasonal, which means the restaurant is empty during the low season. Local customers mean continuity, but the locals are also critical and more difficult to please. It sometimes seems as if we have to take an exam almost every day! But it keeps you alert, and we love it.'

Jurgen Boodie and Abygail Jap-A-Joe in their JiJi's Restaurant, opened with a loan from the Suritrust. In 2013 they received a significant regional award. 'A huge boost that sustains our belief in what we do', says the enterprising couple. Collection JiJi's Restaurant

Helen Piqué

For ten years, Helen Piqué (55) has provided transportation for school children. She now owns two buses. She asked for her first loan in 2011, through the Women's Business Group (WBG). She did so on the advice of a friend after telling her that she could not afford the upkeep of her old bus. She was surprised by how smoothly subsequent events unfolded, and received her first loan. She used this to give her bus a much-needed service: new tires, a complete overhaul of the chassis, the body re-sprayed. 'Since then, I apply for a loan there every year. After all, my coaches have to be ready to use a week before school begins.'

She repaid the three loans she has taken on time. The monthly repayments aren't a problem, according to Piqué. 'You decide how many instalments you want. They calculate the costs for you: if you want to repay it in six months, this is the amount; if you want to pay it back over nine months, then it is this much. You decide what is best for you.' She is also pleased with the WBG's guidance. 'They also teach you how to do the administration.'

Her vehicles transport over 60 children daily. Two rides in the morning and another two in the afternoon, when school finishes. Her first trip, at seven o'clock in the morning, is to drop off preschoolers and primary school children, followed by the advanced elementary and secondary school students. Her early shift ends at five to eight. Then everything starts again at a quarter past eleven in reverse order, and by a quarter past two, all the children have been collected and dropped off. 'I love children,' she says, 'I get along with them really well. I host a big Christmas dinner for them at my house every year, and all the children attend.'

Piqué wants to do this work for a few more years until she turns 60. She encourages her two daughters to take over the business. One of them is already on board – she drives the second bus. Later this year, Piqué will apply for a loan to purchase a third bus – then there will be one for her other daughter to drive too.

Chandra Binnendijk studied journalism and works as an independent editor in Suriname. She has been involved as co-author and editor in a number of publications about Suriname's culture, history and visual arts.

De Surinaamsche Bank has always played an active role in supporting the arts. These security grilles protecting the windows of the DSB building were designed by Erwin de Vries (also see p. 142ff.).
Collection KITLV

Inderill
Junior

6 ory

15.00 Eyma

255 years of paper money in Suriname

Surinamese bank and currency notes from 1760 to 2014

Theo van Elmpt

Paper currency in Suriname is an important economic tool of everyday life, but it is also a reflection of important moments in the country's political and economic history. For example, the abolition of slavery in 1863 and, more recently, the revolution of 1980, have been echoed in the images on the paper money. Even elements of Suriname's diverse culture, natural wealth, and industrial power have been depicted over the years.

Many Surinamese banknotes of a later date are graphic artworks, highlights of illustrative techniques at the time they were produced, but they evolved from far simpler beginnings. During the first hundred years of the colony, there was no paper currency and copper coins and sugar (among other things) were used in transactions and trade. Later, as trade expanded, silver coins were also supplied from the Netherlands. The value of the currency was expressed in guilders: one guilder could be divided into 20 stivers. Besides the guilder, foreign silver and gold coins were also frequently used as mediums of exchange. This chapter relates the history of paper currency in Suriname.

Card money

The very limited economic growth until 1750 meant that there was little need for large amounts of cash in the colony. For daily requirements copper and silver coins especially minted for Suriname were mainly used. As the economy deteriorated, these were hoarded or disappeared abroad, with a resulting shortage of small-denomination coins.

Governor Wigbold Crommelin (act. 1757-68) suggested solving this problem by issuing lead coins. These had very little intrinsic value and were therefore less attractive to hoard. At that time the governor was the highest authority in the colony, but his power was significantly curtailed by the Court of Police, also called the Political Council, which

Card money with a value of ƒ 5 issued in 1813 and signed by Friderici Jr and Eyma. Collection Nationaal Museum van Wereldculturen, TM 1315-2

had to be consulted on all important decisions. The Court consisted mainly of white plantation owners who were unimpressed by Crommelin's idea of circulating lead coins, and rejected his proposal outright.

Eventually paper money was issued in the form of signed and stamped cardboard coins. This was a form of paper money that had been used in Canada, from 1685 to 1759, where it had been a great success. Cardboard '10-guilder coins' – made from playing cards – were introduced in 1760 in Suriname. These issues were covered by bills of exchange drawn on the Netherlands that were withdrawn as the cardboard coins were withdrawn. In this way the value of these coins was guaranteed and no unsecured currency was in circulation.

Two examples of card money from 1826. The values of these relatively late issues are unknown, but they are probably ƒ 1 and 10 stivers (right) and ƒ 1 (left). Playing cards were replaced with cardboard for later issues.
Collection De Nederlandsche Bank

This experiment was very successful and, on 19 May 1761, the Court decided to alleviate the chronic shortage of small-denomination coins by issuing even more card money. During the first few years, only card money with relatively high face values of 10 guilders and 2:10 guilders (two guilders and 10 stivers, or 2.50 guilders) was issued. Initially, this card money and the silver and copper coins already in circulation satisfied requirements. But soon more and more coins disappeared from use because the population hoarded them: first the silver coins and later the copper.

A practical solution

The card money, which was made from real playing cards, had unprecedented benefits. It was colourful and therefore easily recognisable: a major advantage for a largely illiterate population. The cardboard they were made from was also more resistant to the tropical climate in Suriname than regular paper. Moreover, it was fairly inexpensive and had no intrinsic value, so hoarding it was pointless.

One snag, of course, was that anyone with a deck of cards could be tempted to issue money. To prevent this, card money was distinguished in several ways. Firstly, the (blank) back of the card was marked with a value and a serial number for each issue. Cards also bore the signatures of two members of the Court of Police or the Receiver of Taxes.

To further thwart falsification, the cards were also embossed with the seal of Suriname. In the beginning it was the seal of the Chartered Company of Suriname, consisting of a combination of the arms of the West India Company (WIC), the City of Amsterdam and the arms of the Van Aerssen van Sommelsdijck family, who jointly owned the colony. But in 1795 this was replaced by the seal of the 'Council for the Colonies in America and the Possessions of the State in Africa'. This Council took over the administration of the colony from the WIC, which went bankrupt in 1792. The seal consisted of a three-masted ship carried on a shield by two indigenous warriors, and it would form the basis of all additional Surinamese seals and coats of arms. For a short period (1803–4) the seal of the Batavian Republic was used, but from 1805 the 'Council for the Colonies' seal was used again. This would continue until 1826, the year the last of the card money was issued.

Cards as coins

When the currency was first issued, attempts were made to have the card money resemble coins as much as possible. Hence the issues in 1760 of paper discs cut from playing cards that were shaped as coins with a diameter of 38 millimetres, about the size of a Dutch rix-dollar. These discs were worth 10 guilders. Cutting them out soon became impractical and was not very efficient either because, at best, only two coins could be cut from one playing card. Therefore, after 1760 the cards, with a few exceptions, were cut into smaller pieces to create lower denomination currency.

The increasing number of issues resulted in a shortage of playing cards, so plain paper of the same dimensions was used. But this introduced a degree of chaos to the system because, for some issues, ordinary cardboard playing cards were also used for the same values. The choice was probably determined by what was available at that time in the colony.

After the first issues, the cards were often rectangular in shape. The value was indicated by cutting off part of a card (or not). A whole card with two embossed stamps was generally worth 10 guilders and was therefore called *bigi karta* (large card). But there were also three-quarter cards with a value of one guilder (or four shillings) and half cards of 50 cents (two shillings). This system was not consistent, because there were also half cards of one guilder. Again, this was probably caused by the number of playing cards available at any given time. A multitude of sizes and shapes of card money was issued throughout the years.

The economic potential of card money

Initially, card money only served as a medium of exchange, but the colonial administration soon discovered that they could issue card money to create capital to reinvigorate the economy. The first issues were sporadic and did not exceed 25,000 guilders per year, but the frequency quickly intensified and later, amounts of 600,000 guilders per year were no exception. Although many of the issues were supposed to replace old, unusable cards, it did eventually lead to a net increase of unsecured currency and thus inflation.

Besides the card money, from 1772 so-called bonds or government loans were issued to cater to demands for larger amounts. These bonds were soon treated as paper money. Slave owners were even legally obliged to accept these bonds as payment when the government rented their slaves. To ensure that the total amount of 'money' in circulation did not get out of control, bond issues were frequently accompanied by the withdrawal and destruction of an equal amount of card money. Early bonds still paid an interest rate of 5 per cent but in 1796, the government could no longer afford this and decided that the bonds could only be redeemed at face value.

Private issues

Until 1763, the lowest denomination card was 2.50 guilders. This was a relatively high amount, but the opinion was that, together with the coins already in circulation, the daily need for coins would thus be adequately covered. But the more card money there was in circulation, the more the copper and silver coins were hoarded and the greater the need for small change. Yet, the Court initially refused to issue card money with lower denominations.

The local merchants took advantage of this situation by issuing paper 'money' in the form of coupons. These private issues were often printed on very cheap paper and looked as if they had been made with a potato stamp. It is therefore not surprising that almost no examples appear to have survived through the years. These notes lacked any form of security and were therefore quickly and widely copied. Shopkeepers often refused to accept them and, when it suited them, also rejected the real notes, declaring them forgeries. This led to the Court receiving a torrent of complaints and lawsuits from people who considered themselves wronged. On 21 May 1771, the Court banned private issues and card money was issued in lower denominations to prevent further inconvenience.

Paper money from the General Society

From 1799 to 1816 English rule was reimposed, under the so-called British Interim Government with the exception of a brief period in the Napoleonic era (1802–4). Although Napoleon was defeated in 1812, it would take another four years and much wrangling before the English returned Suriname to the Netherlands. The issuing of card money and bonds continued under English control and after 1820 the new Dutch colonial government also issued card money.

At that time it very quickly became clear that drastic measures were needed to harness the worsening economy. Therefore, in 1827, all card money and bonds were withdrawn and replaced by real banknotes. The board now had to decide if it would print and issue banknotes itself, the problem being that there was no Surinamese government or central bank to perform this task. A partnership was therefore sought with an issuing bank in the Netherlands.

Two such banks existed at the time. Both had the right to issue banknotes based on a charter of King William I. The Nederlandsche Bank – which was set up at the instigation of King William I – issued banknotes in the Northern Netherlands. The General Society for the Advancement of National Diligence in Brussels (which would develop into the Société Générale) operated in the Southern Netherlands. Both were allowed to issue paper money that was valid throughout the entire kingdom.

Initially, the government chose to transfer the responsibility for circulating paper money in Suriname to the Nederlandsche Bank. There was even a Royal Decree issued to that effect on 1 January 1827 stating that Dutch money would also be valid in the colony. But it soon became clear that the Nederlandsche Bank was going through a tough period at that time and did not relish the idea of overseeing money circulation in Suriname too. The General Society was not interested either. The colonial government therefore decided to buy a quantity of the General Society's existing notes for Suriname. Preventing these notes from flowing back to the motherland was vital, so they were provided with an orange stamp with the word 'SURINAME'. This solution was obviously much cheaper than having banknotes printed.

Suriname bought a nominal amount totalling two million guilders' worth of banknotes. Besides these banknotes, 400,000 guilders of the General Society's coins were included to completely replace all the card money and coins circulating in the country at the time, a total of 2,096,742 guilders. In return for this, a bill of exchange was issued with a value of 2.4 million guilders, drawn on the Surinamese Treasury, at an interest rate of 5 per cent per annum.

Security
The General Society's banknotes were printed by Johan Enschedé & Sons in Haarlem, the Netherlands. Despite their simple appearance, these notes, printed on one side only, had a large number of security features to help prevent their counterfeiting. One of the most ingenious was the use of the Fleischman 'musical notation' border. This was a very complex border consisting of musical notation elements that were originally carved for Enschedé by Joan Michael Fleischman for printing sheet music. Only Enschedé had these characters, so no other printer could imitate it.

All the banknotes bore a complex serial number and a watermark. The texts and values were indicated in capital letters in different fonts that only Enschedé had. They also bore the signatures of several General Society directors and were countersigned by the administrator of the Colonial Administration, J. Helb.

Paper money issued by the General Society for the Advancement of National Diligence, specially created for use in Suriname by overprinting it with a red text reading 'SURINAME'.
Collection De Nederlandsche Bank

Another ingenious technique was devised to prevent the counterfeiting of notes of one guilder and higher. The left side of the note was a counterfoil with the same number as the banknote. Upon issue this counterfoil was cut off the note with specially serrated scissors and then archived. If a note's authenticity was doubted, the counterfoil was retrieved and if the corrugations of the two pieces fitted exactly, then it was real; if the corrugations did not align then it was clearly a forgery. And if all this was not enough to deter counterfeiters, the notes were also embossed with the name and logo of the General Society. However, these notes would only circulate for three years, from 1826 to 1829.

The Private West India Bank – the oldest bank in the West

In 1828 it was obvious that Suriname's banking system had to be put on a new footing to stimulate economic development in the country. This led to the creation of the Private West India Bank (PWIB) on 9 March 1829. Although the name of the bank suggests that it was a private initiative, it was actually a State bank. The board was formed by the governor of the colony, assisted by a number of senior officials. The new bank was housed in the Waag, which had already been thoroughly renovated and equipped for this purpose with security features such as barred windows. Nevertheless thieves managed to break in a few weeks after the bank opened and get away with some still-unnumbered and unsigned notes. History does not tell us if they were caught.

The PWIB's charter allowed it to issue up to a maximum of three million guilders in banknotes. As security for this issue an equal amount would be borrowed from bankers in the Netherlands. The bank would also receive a subsidy of 150,000 guilders per year from the colonial administration to cover operational costs.

The novelty of the PWIB concept was that its notes could not be exchanged for hard currency, but only against bills of exchange in the Netherlands. This meant that the value of Suriname's paper currency was indeed dependent on confidence in the Dutch monetary system, but that it would not disappear abroad because it could not be used there. This approach differed from issues by other banks at the time because there was no backing in the form of gold or silver and also because the security was limited to a country outside the area where the banknotes circulated.

As with many plans, this one did not work exactly as expected. It proved impossible to convince a banker in the Netherlands to lend the PWIB the three million guilders and ultimately the Dutch government itself had to underwrite this amount. In the meantime, the bank had begun issuing banknotes. These were ordered from Johan Enschedé by the Minister of Colonies and were delivered in January 1829.

The PWIB had already started replacing the General Society's banknotes with its own paper currency in August 1829, long before the loan of three million had been arranged, so the banknotes were basically unsecured. The reason for this haste was obvious. The faster the old notes were removed from circulation, the shorter the period that interest would have to be paid on the outstanding loan from the General Society that formed the security for these notes.

Design and Security

At first glance the PWIB bills seemed simply designed but like the General Society's banknotes they had several safety features. They were printed on one side only, on sheets of sixteen or eight bills, depending on the value. The uncut printed sheets were sent to Suriname where they were numbered, signed, and separated into individual banknotes.

Denominations with a value of 10 guilders and above were provided with the signatures of two of the bank's salaried governors. Notes with a lower value were, in principle, signed by the bank's secretary: obviously he could not do all this work himself, so he appointed a number of officials to assist him – after working hours. The amounts that the officials were paid were proportionate to the number of banknotes they signed.

To combat counterfeiting, the notes were again provided with the Fleischman 'musical notation border'. Tiny deviations were incorporated into these borders on every banknote, which greatly simplified detecting forgeries because counterfeiters usually overlooked them. At that time counterfeiters had no access to photo-reproductive techniques and bills had to be copied by hand. Those who attempted to do this and were caught were dealt with severely. Punishments for falsifying or possessing counterfeit banknotes including flogging, branding and forced labour.

The notes the PWIB issued in 1829 were all square or rectangular and had a black overprint. To simplify the system for the mainly illiterate population, in 1837 other shapes were also introduced, such as a hexagonal banknote, and the different values were

An unsigned and uncut *f* 1 banknote from the West India Private Bank. These notes were cut manually before they were put into circulation.
Collection Stichting Museum Enschedé

also printed in different colours. In 1840 a note worth one guilder had an elongated hexagon shape. The special physical characteristics of the new notes quickly gave rise to the emergence of new Surinamese words like *wan redi-redi* for the fifteen-cent banknote that was printed in red, and *wan skoinsi* (an 'oblique') for the 25-cent note.

An unpleasant end

Although the bank's charter allowed it to issue a total of three million guilders, this was not closely monitored. By 1831 the PWIB had already exceeded the permissible amount by 1,126,000 guilders. Moreover, like many other banks, the PWIB had made the fundamental mistake at the time of providing loans against mortgages instead of against items that converted more easily to cash such as jewellery, tobacco, coffee or wood. To make matters worse, the PWIB could no longer count on help from the Dutch government, which was in dire financial straits after the separation of Belgium in 1830 and could no longer provide loans to the PWIB to guarantee further issues.

In 1847 the PWIB could no longer meet its obligations and was declared bankrupt. The bank shut its doors in 1848, but it would take until 1870 before the books were closed and the bill was settled in full. Despite its brief existence, the PWIB's banknotes can be seen as the first true Surinamese paper currency, issued for use in Suriname by a specially created Surinamese issuing bank.

De Surinaamsche Bank

The proportion of Suriname's population that had money to spend was relatively low in the first half of the nineteenth century. The majority of the population consisted of slaves without any disposable income. Therefore there was no basis for a significant currency circulation. This situation changed dramatically on 1 July 1863, however, when more than 34,000 slaves were freed. Plantation owners were paid a compensation of 300 guilders per slave. After their release former slaves were obliged by law to continue working on the plantations, but now at a wage. Consequently, the demand for currency increased dramatically. However, without slave labour the plantations proved unprofitable, so many plantation owners increasingly invested their energy and the compensation they received in trade. Since the bankruptcy of the PWIB in 1847 no paper money had been issued in the colony and it was clear that a far better monetary system was now needed. This eventually led to the founding of De Surinaamsche Bank N.V. in 1865.

Simon Abendanon

The creation of De Surinaamsche Bank was largely due to the efforts of Simon Abendanon, a bailiff in Paramaribo. In his daily work, he was confronted with the dire economic situation in Suriname and how it affected residents and small businesses. He had noticed that the situation in neighbouring Demerara was a lot healthier and was convinced that this was largely due to the more developed banking system in that country. But his ideas were not very enthusiastically received by the colonial government, which was uncertain of Suriname's potential as a colony and was definitely not in favour of setting up yet another note-issuing bank. This was not surprising, given the expensive failure of the PWIB.

But Abendanon was a go-getter. He moved with his family to the Netherlands to personally convince the Minister of Colonies of the need to set up a new issuing bank. The Minister, however, was totally uninterested in a new adventure. Eventually, Abendanon decided to find a private sponsor, which he did, quite rapidly, in the person of the Dutch philanthropist and entrepreneur Samuel Sarphati. After several false starts, the pair managed to obtain a charter to found a private issuing bank in Suriname.

The governor of Suriname ratified the charter in 1864, but it was not until 19 January 1865 that the required capital of one million guilders was raised and the bank could be established. The charter was valid for 25 years with the open-ended option to extend it for consecutive periods of 25 years. The bank's head office was registered in Amsterdam and a branch was set up in Paramaribo where the actual banking operations would be carried out.

Abendanon left the Netherlands on 8 April 1865 to assume the post of director-secretary of the new bank in Paramaribo. Accompanied by director Henri Muller, they would oversee the actual establishment of the bank in Paramaribo. Issuing and circulating banknotes had the highest priority, as it would allow the withdrawal of gold and silver coins from circulation. Muller and Abendanon therefore took an initial stock of newly-printed banknotes with them from the Netherlands: bills with face values of 10 guilders (the lowest value that could be issued according to the charter), 25, 50, 100, 200, 300 and 1000 guilders.

In contrast to the PWIB notes, these banknotes from De Surinaamsche Bank had been comprehensively prepared and only needed a signature and a number: cutting was consigned to the past. A special machine brought from the Netherlands alleviated the tasks of numbering and signing the banknotes.

Initially the notes were issued only very slowly because the directors were a little uncertain of the prospects. They were concerned that, in the event of a sudden run on the bank it would be unable to exchange the notes for hard cash. However, events unfolded much better than expected and on 19 August 1865 the board in Paramaribo was able to inform the head office that, to its delight, the population was eager to exchange its gold and silver for paper money.

The first banknotes of De Surinaamsche Bank (1865)

The notes that Muller and Abendanon took to Suriname were printed by Johan Enschedé and dated 1 July 1865. They were printed on one side only on cream-coloured paper and had a watermark consisting of the words 'SURINAAMSCHE BANK'. The design drew on the abolition of slavery and consisted of a decorative border containing the Surinamese coat of arms with a female and male warrior (instead of the two male warriors of the current Surinamese coat of arms) and an allegorical depiction of the Dutch Maiden as bringer of civilisation and progress.

The allegory depicts a kneeling slave, casting off his chains, thanking the Dutch Maiden for his freedom. A white plantation owner, standing proudly erect, offers the Maiden the products of the country. Looking back at the dubious role the Netherlands played in the slave trade and the long delay in abolishing slavery in Suriname, this is an ironic image. The Netherlands was certainly not one of the first countries to abolish slavery in its colonies – Great Britain had already done so 1833.

Above: Proof of the ƒ 1000 banknote from 1865. These were the first notes De Surinaamsche Bank issued. Collection Stichting Museum Enschedé

Below: A proof of De Surinaamsche Bank's ƒ 5 banknote from 1869. This was the lowest denomination banknote that De Surinaamsche Bank could issue under its charter. Collection De Nederlandsche Bank

It soon became clear, already in the early years of De Surinaamsche Bank's existence, that smaller denomination notes of 2.50 and 5 guilders were required to replace the small coins still in circulation. In 1868, therefore, a new Royal Decree was sought and obtained that allowed for amendments to the existing charter. The first 5-guilder notes, of which 100,000 were printed in November 1869, were circulated in May 1870, and were reprinted several times in the years that followed. However, Suriname would have to wait more than half a century for the 2.50-guilder note.

The First World War: the return of paper coinage

In 1829, the 18th-century card money was replaced by silver coins and banknotes issued by the Private West India Bank. It would take until 1918 before a paper equivalent to coins was issued in Suriname again: the *zilverbon* (literally 'silver note'). This was a direct result of the outbreak of the First World War. Although neither Suriname nor the Netherlands was directly involved in the hostilities, the populations in both countries immediately began hoarding silver coins, causing a great scarcity of coinage. The government in the Netherlands was forced to issue more silver currency. But the related costs were so high that the government reverted to the old system of a paper substitute. Thus, the issuing of *zilverbonnen* ('silver notes') in the Netherlands began in 1914. These *zilverbonnen* could be redeemed for silver after the situation had returned to normal.

It was clear that, under these conditions, the Dutch government could no longer provide Suriname (which had the same problems) with silver money. So, in 1918, the Surinamese government asked De Surinaamsche Bank to cooperate on issuing Surinamese *zilverbonnen*. Printed in Suriname from locally manufactured plates, these *zilverbonnen* had values of 50 cents, one guilder and 2.50 guilders. They were clearly emergency issues: short on beauty and without any safety features. Therefore, in 1920 production of the *zilverbonnen* was shifted to De Bussy, a security printer in Amsterdam, which used plates manufactured by Enschedé. As expected, this paper currency was not very popular with the locals. But the government did honour its promise in 1922 and exchanged the *zilverbonnen* printed by De Bussy for silver coin.

Above: The 50-cent *zilverbon* ('silver note') from 1918 that was printed in Suriname with locally made plates.
Collection De Nederlandsche Bank

Below: A ƒ 2.50 *zilverbon* printed by De Bussy with plates manufactured by Enschedé. The colours were deliberately very dark and unclear to help prevent their falsification.
Collection De Nederlandsche Bank

The right to issue coins

In all those years the issuing of coins – whether it was (precious) metal or a paper equivalent – was a right that the government kept to itself, and always would. Neither De Surinaamsche Bank nor the later Central Bank of Suriname could issue coins and, theoretically speaking, they had nothing to do with it. This also applied to the *zilverbonnen*, which were a paper substitute for coins so not actual banknotes but paper coin notes, just like the card money issued in the 18th century. Suriname thus also has one of the oldest traditions when it comes to issuing *zilverbonnen*.

Although they bore no responsibility for issuing coins or *zilverbonnen*, the banks were, in practice, deployed by the government – the Ministry of Finance – to handle their introduction into circulation because the Ministry did not have the organisation to do this. These tasks consisted of putting and keeping the coins in circulation and also removing them from circulation again when they were worn out or if an issue was withdrawn. On balance, this also applied to the *zilverbonnen*.

The banks were not always happy with this situation, because putting these notes into circulation and maintaining them was a rather burdensome task – much more so than keeping banknotes in circulation – and they received no compensation. In practice, however, the banks offered little resistance because they were dependent on the government to obtain the bank charter that allowed them to operate.

A radical new design (1920)

The original 1865 banknote design was replicated many times until 1919. The only modifications were new functional job titles and signatures, which changed whenever new management was installed. In 1919 the bank started experimenting with pre-printed note numbers and double-sided printing. These experiments were very successful and led to the decision in 1920 to have the notes radically redesigned. The existing design, based on the abolition of slavery, was no longer considered relevant. Moreover, thanks to the growing availability of photo-reproduction techniques, forgery had become considerably simpler.

The new design was much more complex and included vignettes depicting rice farming, mining, forestry, and fishing, emphasising the importance of these sectors for Suriname. Notes were designed for the already existing denominations of 10, 25, 50, 100, 200, 300, and 1000 guilders.

The new banknotes were very different from the existing ones. Not only were they printed on both sides, they were also pre-numbered, featured pre-printed signatures, and each value had its own colour scheme. Moreover, thanks to the very detailed engravings and images, the new designs were much more difficult to forge. There was no new design for the 5-guilder note, which continued to circulate in its old form mainly because counterfeiters were not interested in this low value and the bank did not think a new design was necessary.

The different values of the new design were not introduced simultaneously but were spread over several years, as and when the need to reissue new banknotes arose. The bank had a very tight spending policy, so it

A proof of De Surinaamsche Bank's ƒ 10 banknote from 1920. This was the first truly new design since 1865.
Collection ABN/AMRO

kept expenses to a minimum. As a natural consequence, the original design was never significantly altered.

The *angisa* design (1935)

When in 1935 a new supply of 5-guilder notes was needed, the bank took the opportunity to have them redesigned as well. The existing version had been in use since 1869 and was virtually unaltered, so it did not convey the modern image the bank wanted to project. To inspire printer Enschedé with the design, the bank sent the company two photographs of Surinamese women wearing the characteristic Surinamese headscarf, the *angisa*. This headdress was folded into many different shapes and was part of the *kotomisi* – the typically national attire worn by Surinamese women at the time.

However, what the Amsterdam-based directorate had not taken into account was that the lovely and innocent-looking *angisa* was also used to express the mood of the person wearing it. This was a custom dating back to the times of slavery, when women used it to communicate with each other without their masters noticing. While the management in Amsterdam was aware of this tradition, they had no idea what the *angisas* on the photos expressed. The image the printer eventually chose meant something along the lines of 'So what, who cares' – not quite the message the bank wanted on its banknotes. When the Paramaribo management pointed this out at the last minute, Enschedé only barely managed to replace the picture with another one.

That the new image, which was used, carried an equally colourful message – 'I'm the life and soul of the party' – went unnoticed by everyone at the bank. Compared to the 1869 design, the new *angisa* banknote was rather complex, featuring much fine engraving and a dark colour scheme to make forgery more problematic.

De Surinaamsche Bank's ƒ 5 banknote of 1935. The motif was the *angisa*, the colourful and imaginatively folded headdress that was part of the local costume. Private collection

The Second World War and the American notes (1941)

Fortunately, the *angisa* banknotes, which were in very high demand, could be shipped to Suriname just before the Second World War broke out and were put into circulation immediately. As it happened, the war had major consequences for De Surinaamsche Bank. Communication between the head office in Amsterdam and the actual bank in Paramaribo became impossible. As an emergency measure, a Royal Decree was rapidly issued that made the bank in Paramaribo an independent legal entity, with its official office registered in the capital of Suriname. Furthermore, the bank could no longer order new banknotes from Enschedé, so it had to look for a new supplier.

An alternative was soon found in the American Bank Note Company (ABNC) in New York. The ABNC would remain the supplier of Surinamese banknotes throughout the Second World War and beyond. The war led to a great shortage of silver coinage, as the population quickly started hoarding it. The 2.50-guilder coin in particular soon disappeared from circulation. The bank then decided to issue notes with this value. Although they were ordered from the ABNC immediately, it took some time before they were finally delivered. In the meantime, the bank decided to cut the existing *angisa* notes in two and issue each half as a 2.50-guilder note. The half notes were marked on both sides with a red stamp as a 2.50-guilder note.

The banknotes ordered from the ABNC looked completely different from the rather conservative designs printed by Enschedé in the Netherlands. They were colourful and featured a large, allegorical image in the centre. The notes were put into circulation immediately upon delivery and the emergency half 5-guilder notes were withdrawn at the same time.

The bank was very happy with the ABNC designs, which were much more colourful and modern than the Enschedé ones. Additionally, they found the paper the ABNC used of much higher quality. However, the American notes had significantly fewer safety features and in practice it turned out that the paper quality did not make that much of a difference. In spite of this, the bank would retain the ABNC as a supplier until long after the war, even though getting in contact with Enschedé after 1945 was no longer a problem.

De Surinaamsche Bank's ƒ 2.50 emergency note of 1939. Collection De Nederlandsche Bank

De Surinaamsche Bank's specimen ƒ 100 banknote from 1941. This series of notes, with the Presidential Palace as a main motif, was printed by the American Banknote Company in New York. Enschedé was not accessible because of the war. Private collection

The Second World War – the return of *zilverbonnen*

Just like during the First World War (1914–18), the Second World War made the issuing of silver coinage complicated. It was again impossible to export silver from the Netherlands and, for the second time, the Surinamese government was forced to issue paper *zilverbonnen* instead of silver coins. As before, the *zilverbonnen*, dated 1940, were backed with the promise that they would be exchanged for the real thing as soon as the situation normalised.

A 50-cent *zilverbon* ('silver note') from 1940, printed by the American Banknote Company in New York because the war had severed communications with Enschedé. Private collection

Like De Surinaamsche Bank's banknotes at the time, the *zilverbonnen* were printed by the ABNC. However, only 50-cent and 1-guilder notes were issued this time. De Surinaamsche Bank had already exercised its mandate to issue 2.50-guilder notes and there would be considerable confusion if both *zilverbonnen* and banknotes with this value circulated simultaneously.

Because silver remained scarce even after the war, the government continued to issue paper *zilverbonnen*. Under the new 1949 charter of De Surinaamsche Bank it was no longer allowed to issue 2.50-guilder notes, which gave the government the opportunity to issue *zilverbonnen* with that value in 1950. In this way it intended to prevent further hoarding of the modest amount of silver coinage still in circulation. These new *zilverbonnen* were once again printed by Enschedé, much to the dismay of De Surinaamsche Bank, which was very satisfied with the designs and quality of the ABNC's *zilverbonnen*.

A ƒ 2.50 *zilverbon* from 1950 with the Roman god of commerce, Mercury, as the central motif. The war had ended, which meant Enschedé could print these notes. Private collection

The Amsterdam notes (1951)

In 1951 the bank added yet another new series to the banknotes already in circulation. They did this not because the latter were no longer suitable, but actually to rescue the Surinamese government from a rather embarrassing situation. The government was planning to set up a central bank, which would release De Surinaamsche Bank of its issuing tasks. It also wanted more control over the issuing of paper money and, most of all, over the profits it generated. However, setting up such an institution turned out to be more complicated than initially thought and the plan to make this new central bank operational from 1953 was delayed considerably.

In itself, this would not have been a problem, had not the minister in charge already ordered new banknotes in 1949 from Amsterdam-based printer De Bussy – ahead of the new bank's foundation. By the time it was clear that the new central bank would not be in place for several more years, the backs of these banknotes had already been printed. Fortunately, they featured no reference to the name of the future central bank (De Bank van Suriname). The minister asked De Surinaamsche Bank to rescue him from

this delicate situation by taking over the partly printed banknotes and finishing and issuing them as De Surinaamsche Bank's notes. The management was not pleased with the design and quality, but agreed to issue them anyway, after some modifications to the front and the change of the name to 'De Surinaamsche Bank' (see the image of the front of the planned 100-guilder banknote).

The 1951 series, consisting of 10, 25, and 100-guilder notes, would be the last one issued by De Surinaamsche Bank. After several false starts, the planned central bank finally opened its doors on 1 April 1957. On that same day, De Surinaamsche Bank transferred to the Centrale Bank van Suriname (Central Bank of Suriname) its issuing task, which it had performed successfully for almost 100 years. It would continue as an independent bank, eventually becoming one of the most successful commercial banks in Suriname.

Above: De Surinaamsche Bank's specimen ƒ 25 banknote from 1951. This note was actually designed for the yet to be established 'De Bank van Suriname N.V.', but at the last moment it was redesigned for De Surinaamsche Bank. Private collection

Below: The 1951 series printing plate. It bears the original name of the yet to be established central bank, 'De Bank van Suriname N.V.'. Because of the delay in setting up this bank, at the last moment it's name was substituted with that of De Surinaamsche Bank. Private Collection

A central bank for Suriname

The colonial government had made plans as early as 1938 to create a central bank to obtain more control over monetary policy and over the stability and circulation of the Surinamese currency. They set up two committees to advise on the need for and the practical consequences of establishing such an institution. However, when the committees published their findings in 1945, they turned out to be completely contradictory. The Houwink Committee felt a central bank was necessary to develop a healthy banking system and attract foreign capital, while the Trip–De Jong Committee argued that there was no need to establish such a bank at that point, based on practical considerations. In true political fashion, the colonial government then decided to follow both committees' advice and create a central bank, 'but not now….'

The extended charter of De Surinaamsche Bank

The charter of De Surinaamsche Bank was valid until 1 January 1950. Consequently, because of the decision made at the time to once again postpone the creation of a central bank, this charter had to be extended once more. The Surinamese government took the opportunity to gain greater control over the circulation activities and, more importantly, to obtain a larger part of the profits thereof. The charter was amended to that purpose and extended by one year until 31 December 1951.

The reason for this very short extension was the passing of a new Banking Law in 1950 that would improve the regulations pertaining to the tasks of an issuing bank. This law would then form the basis for another extension of De Surinaamsche Bank's charter on 1 January 1951, this time for five years, until 1 January 1956. The most important modification to the 1951 charter was the establishment of a banking committee that would coordinate the monetary and financial regulations implemented by De Surinaamsche Bank and the government. Furthermore, the bank's registered office was moved from the Netherlands to Suriname.

The 1951 charter had a two-year notice period, which meant that the Surinamese government could cancel it before 1 January 1954. If it did not cancel, the charter would automatically be extended by another five years until 1 January 1961. Following a 'now-or-never' scenario, the charter was cancelled on 30 December 1953, at the very last minute, with the announcement of the foundation of the Central Bank of Suriname on 2 January 1956. However, it quickly became clear that that date was not very realistic, so the government immediately decided that, if necessary, the charter could be extended after all. This was a wise decision, for not only was the Central Bank not formally established until 24 October 1956, but it would only actually start its issuing activities in April 1957.

Due to all the delays, De Surinaamsche Bank remained responsible for the circulation of paper currency until 1 April 1957. To avoid any conflicts with the Central Bank's articles of association, articles 11 and 21 – which granted this bank the sole right to issue banknotes – were temporarily suspended. On 28 March 1957, the articles in question became operational again. This sequence of events raises the question of whether the first Central Bank-issued banknotes were actually legal currency, as they were dated 2 January 1957: a time when the relevant articles were still suspended.

Dutch lawyer R.W. Groenman was named president of the new Central Bank. Groenman had worked at the Nederlandsche Bank in Amsterdam for nine years before being sent to Pakistan, and later Paraguay, for the International Monetary Fund. His first priorities in Suriname were to set up an organisation for the new bank, hire personnel, and find a suitable location. This location was eventually found at the former showroom of local energy company Overseas Gas and Electricity Company (OGEM), at Waterkant 28 (see Figure 27 – the building at far right). Initially not very impressive, over time, it was converted into the present building, which became more representative as the bank's tasks and personnel expanded.

The former showroom of the local electricity company on Waterkant in Paramaribo. This is where the Central Bank of Suriname was established in 1957. This property was later redeveloped nto the imposing bank building, which now characterises the appearance of Waterkant. Collection Central Bank of Suriname

The current headquarters of the Central Bank of Suriname on Waterkant in Paramaribo.
Private collection

The first banknotes issued by the Central Bank (1957)

Enschedé printed the first banknotes issued by the Central Bank of Suriname. This happened much to the dismay of the Surinamese Secretary of Finance, S.D. Emanuels, who felt the ABNC notes were much more beautiful and better. Initially, the secretary wanted a series of notes featuring images of freedom fighters such as William of Orange and Simón Bolívar. But this desire to make a political statement quickly faded and he liked Enschedé's proposed designs – with a local flavour – so much that he eventually chose those.

The government selected 2 January 1957 as the issuing date, because 1 January was a Sunday and the secretary was not sure if that was a valid date with regard to the Banking Law. The notes were issued with the values 5, 10, 25, 100, and 1000 guilders. The design for the two lowest denominations showed a Creole girl wearing a necklace, with a fruit basket on her head. The three higher denominations featured a portrait of a Surinamese woman wearing a fruit necklace. The backs were identical on all notes and featured a complex pattern of engraved lines with the Surinamese coat of arms in the centre. All banknotes bore the signature of the first president of the Central Bank, R.W. Groenman, on the front.

The Central Bank of Suriname's ƒ 1000 banknote from 1957. This was the first series of banknotes issued by the newly established bank. Portraits of Surinamese women were used as motifs. Private collection

When the Central Bank took over De Surinaamsche Bank's issuing responsibilities, the old banknotes were withdrawn from circulation and replaced with the new ones. However, those turned out to be less durable in the Surinamese climate than expected and new reprints had to be ordered. Those notes were identical to the initial ones and could only be distinguished by their serial numbers.

The Central Bank and the *zilverbonnen*

President Groenman of the Central Bank had very outspoken ideas about the issuing of *zilverbonnen* by the Ministry of Finance. He thought that it would be a good idea if the government stopped issuing them and allowed the bank to issue one- and 2.50-guilder notes. Groenman was also horrified by the terrible state of the *zilverbonnen*: he called them 'nothing more than dirty paper' and 'no longer recognisable as currency'. However, the government maintained its hold on the right to issue these *zilverbonnen*, although of course it left the practical work to the bank.

Thus, one of the first tasks the Central Bank tackled was replacing the filthy *zilverbonnen* but to do this, large numbers of new *zilverbonnen* had to be printed beforehand. This applied mainly to the 1-guilder denomination and less so to the 2.50-guilder denomination, as the population had quickly started to exchange them for the 5-guilder banknotes issued by the bank. In 1958, the bank was proud to announce that all the *zilverbonnen* had been replaced and that it 'hoped it had done national health and hygiene a service in doing so, having made the public aware of the need to treat its paper currency with more care'.

The introduction of the Surinamese guilder (1960)

Until 1960, the Surinamese monetary system was measured in Dutch guilders. However, that year a bill was passed aimed at reorganising the entire national monetary system; and at the same time it declared the Surinamese guilder as the national currency. The difference was minimal: instead of the ƒ symbol, now the national currency was officially written as Sƒ. The word 'guilder' remained unchanged on all paper currency.

When the country switched from the Dutch guilder to the Surinamese guilder, the term '*zilverbon*' was replaced with *muntbiljet* ('coin note'). This was a more suitable name, as it better represented what the note actually was: a replacement for coins. However, the *muntbiljet* could no longer be exchanged for silver. The first *muntbiljet* notes were issued in 1961, immediately after the new law became effective. In the years that followed there were several new designs for these notes including, for example, one featuring the Ministry of Finance building as the central image, and another a *kotomisi*.

The 1960 law also allowed for the issue of silver Surinamese guilder coins. This was done to prevent the importation of Dutch guilder coins and partly reduce the issue of *muntbiljetten* ('coin notes'). However, to their surprise, both the government and the bank discovered that the population was not particularly eager to obtain silver Surinamese guilder coins. Apparently, people preferred the paper equivalent, which weighed less and was easy to use. As a consequence, the issuing of *muntbiljetten* grew steadily from 1960. Unfortunately, this was more a sign of growing inflation than of a growing economy. This was not only bad for Suriname, but also for the bank, as it had to put more and more currency notes into circulation, with all the work that this entailed.

In 1963, Groenman resigned as president and was replaced by V.M. de Miranda, a former chartered accountant and head of the Central National Accountants Department in Suriname and one of the few qualified local candidates. After his appointment, new banknotes were issued in 1963 featuring his signature, while Suriname's old coat of arms was replaced with a new design by Lou Lichtveld, as approved by the government in 1960. The front remained identical to that of the 1957 notes, with the exception of the signature. These banknotes would be reprinted without modifications several times until 1981.

Above: A ƒ 1 *muntbiljet* ('coin note') from 1965 with the Ministry of Finance building in Paramaribo as the main motif. Private collection

Below: The ƒ 2.50 *muntbiljet* from 1973. These notes were printed by Bradbury Wilkinson in England because the bank found Enschedé too expensive and the quality of their paper inferior. Private collection

The Revolution series (1982)

In 1980 there was a military coup in Suriname and a revolutionary government that was firmly under the control of the army took over power. When the political situation changed after the coup, on 1 December 1980 economist Jules Sedney was appointed as president of the Central Bank. The banknotes were modified as well and, although the changes were made within the existing design, their message was significant. On the front, the motif of the girls was replaced by an image of the Monument of the Revolution, designed by Surinamese artist Jules Chin A Foeng. This was done in part because reluctance had grown against the depiction of indigenous faces on account of possible political sensibilities and the monument was seen as a more neutral option. On the back, the coat of arms featuring the text *'Justitia, Pietas, Fides'* (*'Justice, Piety, Fidelity'*) was no longer found fitting and was replaced with an image of the Presidential Palace. The year 1982 saw the 25th anniversary of the Central Bank and Sedney wanted to depict the Central Bank building on some of the banknotes as well. At the time, Enschedé was unable to handle the extra work and it was ultimately decided to print the Presidential Palace on all the banknotes. These would be the last banknotes printed by Enschedé for a while.

Central element of the Monument of the Revolution in Paramaribo, designed by Jules Chin A Foeng. This motif was used in the design of the series of banknotes issued by the Central Bank of Suriname in 1982.
Private collection

The end of the collaboration with Enschedé

In the 1970s the long-standing relationship between Suriname and Enschedé was severely disrupted when the Central Bank found out that the printer had been making large concessions to other countries when it came to prices, but not to Suriname. In addition to the frequent complaints about the quality of the paper, this was reason enough for the bank to order the 2.50-guilder notes from English printer Bradbury Wilkinson from 1978.

Following the execution of fifteen critics of the military regime in December 1982 (the so-called December Murders), the Netherlands suspended its development aid to the country and consequently many Dutch trading partners, including Enschedé, fell out of favour in Suriname. This led to a break in the over century-long collaboration with Enschedé. Eventually, from 1983 this resulted in the Central Bank having all bank and currency notes printed by English printer Thomas de la Rue (which had since taken over Bradbury Wilkinson). The 1982 banknotes, the Revolution series, were still delivered by Enschedé, as their production had already started at the time the collaboration ended.

Galloping inflation

After the coup, economic chaos ensued that caused inflation to spin completely out of control. This caused the banknotes from the so-called Revolution series to decrease rapidly in value. Sedney had been replaced in 1983 by interim president W. Lieuw A Soe who managed to guide the bank through several difficult years, until Henk Otmar Goedschalk was appointed as the new president in 1985. Because Lieuw A Soe was interim president, his signature was not on any banknote reprints and the old Revolution notes, signed by Sedney, remained in circulation for the duration of his tenure.

Goedschalk, a Surinamese economist educated in the Netherlands, tried to impose order on the widespread monetary and economic chaos. One of the first problems he tackled was changing the Revolution notes. They had been in use for several years already and had become so grubby that they were considered a health risk. Goedschalk had a number of banknotes from the Revolution series reprinted, with his signature, to replace those signed by Sedney.

The Central Bank of Suriname's Sƒ 10 banknote from 1982. The design was based on the Monument of the Revolution and not on portraits of local beauties. Private collection

The Anton de Kom series (1986)

Meanwhile, the Central Bank was secretly preparing wide-reaching currency reforms to quell the rampant black market trade. These became effective on the night of 9 November 1986. The population was allowed only a few days to exchange the old banknotes for notes from a completely new series. Although measures had been taken to keep the preparations secret, the action was by no means as effective as it should have been, as the plans had been leaked prematurely.

As a central theme, this series had the portrait of Anton de Kom, the Surinamese nationalist and resistance hero who, during the Second World War, had been a member of the Dutch resistance. In November 1944 he was arrested by the Nazis in Amsterdam and taken to the Neuengamme concentration camp, where he died on 24 April 1945, a few weeks before the end of the war. Because Enschedé was out of favour, Thomas de la Rue printed these banknotes as well.

All the notes from the De Kom series had the same design, the only difference between them being the colour schemes and values. Banknotes in this series had face values of 5, 10, 25, 100, and 500 guilders. The De Kom series would be reprinted several times, with the addition of a 250-guilder note in 1988.

The Central Bank of Suriname's 100-guilder banknote from the Anton de Kom series of 1986. Depicting the resistance hero was not to everyone's taste and the series was replaced in 1991 by one with a different design.
Private collection

Currency notes replaced with coins

The severe inflation in the 1980s made it clear that the period of imagined wealth in Suriname was over. The number of currency notes had doubled between 1983 and 1987 and the issuing and circulation costs had started to exceed the notes' actual value. It was therefore not surprising that the government eventually ended the issue of this 'paper money' and started replacing the notes with coins made of a copper-nickel alloy. Although these were expensive to manufacture, their lifespan was almost unlimited, which could not be said of paper currency. Therefore it was not long before the last currency note disappeared from circulation.

The Performance series (1991)

Not everybody in Suriname appreciated the De Kom design. Several communities felt misrepresented and protested against the depiction of a national hero who was not acknowledged as such by everyone. For that reason, a new series of banknotes was designed in 1991, this time with the more neutral theme of Surinamese achievements in the areas of sport and the economy. This Performance series was again printed by Thomas de la Rue and initially consisted of the values 5, 10, 25, 100 and 500 guilders. Under pressure of the ever-growing inflation, a 1000-guilder note was added in 1993.

The Central Bank of Suriname's 500-guilder banknote from the 1991 series. The resistance hero used on the 1986 series was replaced with more neutral images of the Bank's building and of sporting and economic activities. Private collection

Due to a change in the political composition of the administration, André Telting replaced Henk Goedschalk as president of the Central Bank in 1994. Normally this would lead to a new batch of banknotes featuring the new president's signature, but it so happened that a large number of new banknotes with Goedschalk's signature had been ordered and produced in 1993. Telting felt it would be financially irresponsible to destroy them and have new ones. It wasn't until 1995, therefore, that 5, 10, 25 and 1000-guilder banknotes bearing Telting's signature were printed. The design of those notes did not change but, driven by the ever-mounting inflation, a new 2000-guilder banknote was added to the series.

After the change of government in 1997, Telting resigned as president of the Central Bank and was immediately succeeded by Henk Goedschalk again. Goedschalk further expanded the series in 1997 with new 5000 and 10,000-guilder notes bearing his signature. Although the design of these high denomination banknotes was vaguely similar to that of the lower denominations, the new notes were much more colourful and featured several, very-advanced, anti-forgery features. In 1998 Goedschalk also had the lower values reprinted with his signature.

The Flora and Fauna series (2000)

In the meantime, the bank had requested a completely new series design from Thomas de la Rue, to replace the mishmash in circulation at that point. The resulting series, inspired by the beautiful flora and fauna of Suriname, is internationally regarded as one of the most beautiful series of banknotes. No effort was too great and no expense was spared in its production.

Using advanced techniques, the banknotes were equipped with a number of characteristics that would make convincing forgery virtually impossible. One of the most striking features was a hologram on the 1000 guilder and higher denomination notes. These were brought into circulation in 2000, with Goedschalk's signature. However, that same year, another change of government caused Goedschalk to be replaced by André Telting, who became president of the Central Bank for a second time. Yet again, Telting was confronted with a large quantity of new banknotes signed by his predecessor and, as before, he kept these notes in circulation.

The 10,0000-guilder banknote from the series for the year 2000. This remarkable series has beautiful images of Surinamese birds. It is still the most colourful series in the history of Surinamese banknotes and one of the first in the world with such a bold design. Private collection

Goodbye to the guilder

In 2004 another series appeared with a completely new design. This time, the reason was of a more fundamental nature than at any time before: the currency changed from Surinamese guilders to Surinamese dollars. This change had been considered several times since Suriname's independence in 1975, yet never acted upon. In view of the ever-increasing integration of the Surinamese economy with those of the surrounding countries in the Caribbean and the increasing detachment between Suriname and the former motherland, dollarisation was finally realised in 2004.

With the issue of the dollar notes the government also took the opportunity to reduce the value of high denomination banknotes of 5000 and 25,000 guilders (issued because of the increasing inflation) by eliminating three zeros. Only the banknotes issued by the Central Bank were affected by this revaluation, not the currency notes or coins. Therefore, a Surinamese guilder coin or currency note was still worth a Surinamese dollar (SRD), while a 5000-guilder note was now worth five Surinamese dollars.

The SRD 50 banknote from the 2004 series, printed in Canada by the Canadian Banknote Company.
Private collection

The Surinamese dollar notes were designed and printed by the Canadian Banknote Company. Considerations regarding the necessary protection, and the accompanying costs, led to a very austere series with a design based on the natural beauty of Suriname's landscape. As before, the notes included a large number of security features, but this time they matched the banknotes' true economic value. So, the holograms and other very costly security features used in the 2000 series disappeared. The cost of manufacturing Suriname's paper money was now proportionate to its economic value.

The reintroduction of the *muntbiljet*

Apart from the introduction of the Surinamese dollar, 2004 also saw the return of the *muntbiljet*. This was a consequence of the change to the currency and the relatively high value of the banknotes in circulation at the time, which created a need for low-value notes. For that reason, on 1 January 2004 new notes were issued with the values of 1 SRD and 2.50 SRD. For the first time since 1982 Johan Enschedé in Haarlem printed these notes and revived the very sober designs for the *zilverbonnen* printed by Enschedé in 1949 and 1950, although the colours were much clearer. Hoarded coins and those in bank vaults when the new currency notes were issued remained legal currency and were revalued. The value of a 100-cent coin was changed from a Surinamese guilder to 1 SRD. Quarters, 10-cent pieces, and square stivers (all featuring the Surinamese coat of arms) came back into circulation. This was, after all, cheaper than minting new coins.

The NLG 2.50 *muntbiljet* from 2004. This note, once again designed and printed by Enschedé, has the same austere look as the 2004 banknotes that were printed in Canada.
Private collection

The building on Gravenstraat in Paramaribo where De Surinaamsche Bank began operating in 1865.
Collection DSB

Literature

Benjamins, H.D. & Joh.F. Snelleman (eds.), *Encyclopaedie van Nederlandsch West-Indie*. Amsterdam: S. Emmering, 1981. (Unrevised reprint of 1914–17 edition).

Bruyning, C.F.A. & J. Voorhoeve (eds.), *Encyclopedie van Suriname*. Amsterdam/Brussel: Elsevier, 1977.

Central Bank of Suriname, Annual Reports 1957–98.

De Surinaamsche Bank N.V., Annual Reports 1865–1957. Amsterdam/Paramaribo: De Surinaamsche Bank N.V.

Elmpt, T.F.A. van, *Surinam Paper Currency. Volume 1: 1760 to 1957*. Uithoorn: Elran Press, 1997.

Elmpt, T.F.A. van, *Surinam Paper Currency. Volume 2: 1957 to 2000*. Uithoorn: Elran Press, 2003.

Elmpt, T.F.A. van, *Surinam Paper Currency. Volume 3: Treasury Notes*. Uithoorn: Elran Press, 2000.

Schiltkamp, J.A. & J.Th. de Smidt, *West Indisch Plakaatboek: Plakaten, ordonnantiën en andere wetten, uitgevaardigd in Suriname 1667-1816*, 2 vols., Amsterdam: S. Emmering, 1973.

Theo van Elmpt studied Information Sciences and English Language and Literature. He held various ICT management positions in global organisations, but has always had a keen interest in the design, printing and production aspects of paper currency. He has published a number of books and articles on the paper currency of Suriname, the Netherlands Antilles and British Military banknote issues. He is currently researching the monetary history and paper currency of the former Netherlands East Indies.

The art collection of De Surinaamsche Bank

A collection to be proud of

Marieke Visser

Art collections are an important component of a lively arts and culture sector anywhere in the world. For artists, to have their work included in a collection means having a new source of income, a platform for their work to shine, and also prestige. For the collector, motives vary from pure aesthetic pleasure to a good investment.

Suriname is home to a number of visual art collections, owned by private persons and corporations. A lot of art becomes part of private collections, and thus generally inaccessible for the public. Sometimes, the work is moved abroad, disappearing forever from the nation's view. Corporate art collections are seen by more people. Of course, a painting hanging on a boardroom wall will probably not be seen as often as a sculpture in a reception area, but it is a fact that works in a corporate collection are more visible than those in a private one. For Suriname's art world, the existence of such corporate collections is additionally important, because of the lack of institutions such as a museum of visual arts, or a national gallery. Those who wish to see – or exhibit – art have to resort to a limited circuit of small galleries, exhibition spaces, the three training centres in the country, or the artist's own home or studio.

Art connoisseurs regard the art collection owned by De Surinaamsche Bank N.V. (DSB) as the most beautiful, extensive, balanced and well-maintained corporate collection in Suriname. The foundations for the collection were laid in the early 1970s. This chapter paints a picture of DSB's art collection and its significance for Suriname through the years.

Corporate collections in Suriname

When DSB celebrated its 140th anniversary in 2005, the then board decided to share the collection with a wider audience. This resulted in the *Zichtbaar* (*Visible*) exposition, and a publication of the same name. It was an introduction and an eye-opener for the public, and for other entrepreneurs. Several years later, the Central Bank of Suriname followed with an exhibition and catalogue of its collection: *Talent*. So far, these are the only collections in Suriname that have been (partly) described.

There is always room for art in DSB's offices; this is the painting *Goudkoorts I* ('Gold Rush I') by Rinaldo Klas (see p. 164).
Collection DSB

Among other corporations known to have a collection are the N.V. Energiebedrijven Suriname (EBS), BDO Suriname, the Surinaamsche Waterleiding Maatschappij (SWM), Staatsolie (State Oil), Assuria, Self Reliance, and Fatum. Unlike some corporate collections in Suriname, the DSB collection continues to expand, as a 'living' collection. The bank acquires and receives older works as well. In fact, the DSB collection functions as a State collection. Each work is registered and tracked, and all the works are well maintained. This is the first step towards making the collection permanently accessible to a wider audience.

The origins of the DSB collection

The foundation

DSB president Jozef Brahim and his artistically minded advisor, Rudi de la Fuente, midwifed the bank's art collection. Poet Orlando Emanuels helped them, and together they laid a strong foundation for the art collection, starting in 1971. The bank acquired pieces from the likes of Hans Lie, Stuart Robles de Medina, and Cliff San A Jong. At the time, Nola Hatterman's Art Academy started producing its first results, and the idea was to support young artists.

Though the idea of a corporation collecting art was new, Brahim and his partners' enthusiasm was contagious. Both management and the board of supervisory directors recognised the beauty of the art works the bank was acquiring, and they gradually became aware of the struggle that especially young artists can endure, financially speaking, and who deserve support. This is why DSB started to allocate a fixed amount in their yearly budget to the acquisition of art.

The cover of the book *Zichtbaar*, published in 2005, which accompanied an exhibition of DSB's art collection.
Collection DSB

Director Brahim regularly visited exhibitions, and always kept an eye open for interesting works to acquire for the bank's collection. Brahim's personal taste – rather classical, not abstract, and definitely no multimedia pieces – is evident when reviewing the selection from that early period. But he readily accepted the advice of De la Fuente, whose vision he highly appreciated, and Emanuels, too, made his contributions. When hiring De la Fuente, Brahim had been slightly reluctant: would it all not be too expensive, would this artistic all-rounder not go too far? However, the collaboration was a success from the start.

Rudi de la Fuente

Rudi de la Fuente (1934–2000) was Jozef Brahim's main creative ally. His influence on the DSB art collection, and the company's artistic image, was considerable. Moreover, thanks to him, the awareness of the value of art took root as well.

De la Fuente was first and foremost a graphic artist and designer, but he applied his talents to other artistic pursuits too, including the beautiful cover designs he made for literary magazine *Moetete* and Orlando Emanuels' poetry anthology *Getuige à decharge*. He was also a gifted painter.

Rudi de la Fuente founded the National Institute for Art and Culture Foundation (NIKK) with Jules Chin A Foeng in 1967. In 1981, with Chin A Foeng as director, the foundation merged into the Suriname School of Fine Arts, now known as the Academy for Higher Art and Cultural Education (AHKCO). In 1993, De la Fuente designed the new DSB logo, as well as the distinctive green-purple colour combination.

Partly due to his modesty, De la Fuente's work is unjustly unrecognised in Suriname. This, too, underlines how important it is to have a platform for art that has so far gone unnoticed in private and corporate collections.

The current collection

The better part of the present collection was acquired under director Sigmund Proeve. Since 1999, Henna Rellum has been responsible for the art collection, and its maintenance has become an integral part of her work as general affairs manager. Among her tasks are the administration and maintenance of the collection, the acquisition of new works, and selecting the locations of the works in the bank's various premises. Artist Jules Brand-Flu has been hired to take care of the annual maintenance. He reviews all pieces at least once a year, cleans them, and does minor restorations when necessary. He also advises on acquisitions.

On average, DSB acquires twenty new works each year. Traditionally, acquisitions take place during the National Art Fair, but from time to time the bank is approached when works from an existing collection are being sold, or when pieces become available from an estate. The bank never passes on such once-in-a-lifetime opportunities, even if they sometimes exceed the budget. For example, they bought some marvellous early works by Jules Chin A Foeng, adding to his oeuvre already present in the collection, and with the acquisition of work by Quintus Jan Telting, a piece representing an earlier stylistic period could finally be exhibited.

Ironclad protection and artistic embellishment

Iron window grilles: it can hardly get any more Surinamese than when it comes to the basic protection of a building. Virtually every house and corporate building in the city centre features such window grilles, thwarting thieves, and keeping people and their possessions safe. The marvellous security grilles covering the windows of the DSB building were designed by none other than Surinamese painter and sculptor Erwin de Vries. His design shows that art can be functional too. Or, the other way around: that a necessary evil can also be easy on the eye. In addition, the figures of guardsmen featured in De Vries' wrought ironwork give the whole a symbolic overtone.

The current management places an emphasis on supporting young artists. Recent acquisitions are a perfect example of this. The collection now features work by young talents such as Daniël Lemmer, Kodzo Wilkinson, Ginoh Soerodimedjo, and Shaundell Horton. Furthermore, the bank seeks to have a representative collection. Henna Rellum: 'The bank considers the works of acquired art as an investment, but it is far more important to realise that with these acquisitions we are investing in the promotion and propagation of the visual arts for the long term.'

Visual arts in Suriname

In order to assess the DSB art collection, to understand the historic, economic, and most of all sentimental value of it, we should examine to what extent it reflects the developments in visual arts in Suriname, seeing as there is no leitmotiv or any other guiding criterion when it comes to acquisition. Nevertheless, as you will read in the next section, the collection is a representative cross-section of visual art of the 20th and 21st century. However, before we get to that, we will paint you a picture of the history of art in Suriname.

In search of a starting point

In attempting to pinpoint the genesis of the history of art in Suriname, we immediately have to deal with an issue that is a point of discussion. From a Western viewpoint, the first important steps were made halfway through the 20th century, when three young men moved to the Netherlands to study and discover more about the field of visual arts: Erwin de Vries, Stuart Robles de Medina, and Rudi Getrouw. However, others go back much further in time: to the indigenous cave paintings and petroglyphs; or to the enigmatic mask, presumably pre-Columbian and the only one of its kind in the region, which is now part of the Suriname Museum collection; or the pottery, and, of more recent date, the mythical creatures and other creative and decorative expressions of, for example, the Wayana people. The Maroon people, with their extraordinary woodcarvings known as 'tembe', have also made a great contribution to Suriname's art history. The strong influence of these cultural expressions on Surinamese visual arts can be felt to this day – and perhaps more than ever today. The most famous example is the work of Marcel Pinas, who uses his Ndyuka background as inspiration and motivation, but the same thing also applies to the work of a modern-day artist such as Ken Doorson.

Surinamese visual arts since 1975

At the end of the 20th century, the state of affairs in Surinamese art was documented in the book *Twenty Years of Visual Arts in Suriname 1975-1995*, which accompanied an exhibition. The choice for starting in 1975 was motivated by the fact that much had changed since the year of independence.

One of the most important changes was that Surinamese people no longer went to the Netherlands for an artistic education, but to Jamaica. Rinaldo Klas was the first artist from Suriname to attend Edna Manley College of Visual and Performing Arts on this Caribbean island, in the late 1980s. Many followed, for shorter or longer periods, such as Kenneth Flijders, Wilgo Vijfhoven, Marcel Pinas, George Struikelblok, and Kurt Nahar. This development was important, because it opened new vistas: there was more room to gain entry to and be recognised by the Caribbean identity. Whereas in the past Dutch masters such as Rembrandt and Vermeer were the shining examples to follow, now artists like Jean-Michel Basquiat, an American artist born from the Caribbean diaspora, entered the frame.

The Readytex Art Gallery opened its doors in February 1993. This gallery became – and remains – a tower of strength in times of turmoil with the coming and going of various initiatives, which all contributed to the coming of age of the country's art scene, such as Egi Du, House of Art, Royal House of Art, the Academy for Higher Art and Cultural Education, the Nola Hatterman Art Academy, and the Soeki Irodikromo People's Academy. Another milestone was the foundation of the Federation of Visual Artists in Suriname (FVAS), in October 1998.

The huge coins

René Tosari founded art collective Waka Tjopu in the 1980s. Members of the core group included Steve Ammersingh, Winston van der Bok, Ray Daal, John Djojo, Soeki Irodikromo, René Tosari, and Ramin Wirjomenggolo. Waka Tjopu made enormous replicas of Surinamese coins for DSB, which for a long time were featured on the façade of the main office on Henck Arron Street. They are currently spread around the bank's garden.

Recent developments

The 21st century brought new highlights. The aforementioned exhibitions *Zichtbaar* (2005), and *Talent* (2007), as well as the exhibitions titled *Wakaman – Drawing Lines Connecting Dots* (2009), *Paramaribo SPAN* (2010), and *Kibii Wi Koni Marcel Pinas The Event* (2011) were all unique and groundbreaking exhibitions as well, and all of them were accompanied by a publication.

It is wonderful to see how De Surinaamsche Bank has contributed to this flourishing of the arts. It has continually expanded its art collection, also by including works by young artists and thus ensuring that the collection remains a relevant representation of the scene. It also helped to create room for these developments by collaborating on two exhibitions and publications (*Zichtbaar*, and *Paramaribo SPAN*), and, during Carifesta XI in 2013, immediately offered to host the National Art Fair, which has been held almost yearly since 1965, but after its 2012 edition no longer had a home at the venue Ons Erf.

To conclude, Suriname has also entered the cyberworld of the 21st century. Since 2009, there has been a (mainly) digital platform for visual arts in the country, supported by Readytex Art Gallery: Sranan Art Xposed. A digital magazine, a blog, a digital photo archive, a Facebook page, and other activities are spreading the word about Surinamese visual art at an international level. Furthermore, modern communication techniques have made interaction with artists elsewhere in the world much easier. For example, during the first months of the *Wakaman – Drawing Lines Connecting Dots* project, the collaboration between the interconnected artists took place almost exclusively via the Internet. There was a distinct change after the *Paramaribo SPAN* exhibition, which thanks to the digital highway generated many new projects.

The *Paramaribo SPAN* exhibition was held in DSB's garden. Collection DSB

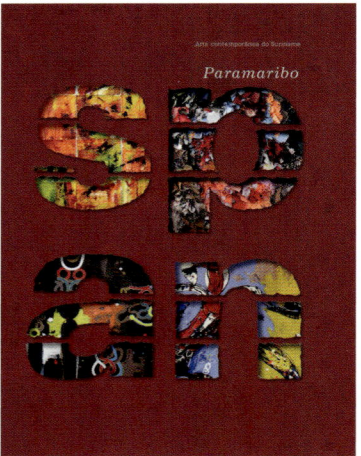

The front cover of the book *Paramaribo SPAN*, that was published in 2000 to mark DSB's 145th anniversary. Collection DSB

The collection in images and word

Together, the art works in in DSB's collection tell the history of Surinamese art over the past 60 years. The following pages contain a selection from its sizeable collection, which includes several hundred objects. More recently acquired works feature here; older pieces can be found in the book *Zichtbaar*.

Erwin de Vries, *Gezicht* ('Face'), mixed media on paper, 53x71 cm, 1987. Acquired 27 June 2006
The DSB collection includes several works by Erwin de Vries: all paintings and aquarelles, except for a bronze bust of national poet Dobru.

There are also several pieces by De Vries' contemporaries Stuart Robles de Medina and Rudi Getrouw. These works are reproduced in *Zichtbaar*.
Artist's website: http://erwindevries.org/

**Jules Chin A Foeng, *untitled*,
oil on linen, 90.5x80 cm, 1974.
Acquired 20 December 2013**

An example of a recent acquisition of an older piece. A good complement to works by Jules Chin A Foeng already in the collection.

Quintus Jan Telting, *Man en hond* ('Man and Dog'), aquarelle and ink on paper, 35x50 cm, 1982. Acquired 20 December 2013

Not a typical Quintus Jan Telting piece, but precisely because of that a surprising acquisition.
Artist's website: http://jantelting.com/

Ro Heilbron, *Maroons of Suriname*, mixed media, 62x62 cm, 2008. Acquired 30 January 2013

Possibly because Ro Heilbron spent many years living on the islands of Saba and St Maarten, the colours in his work often have a Caribbean vibrance. Heilbron's themes vary from women, beauty, and spirituality, to war and struggle: he has frequently depicted the suffering of the indigenous and Maroon peoples.

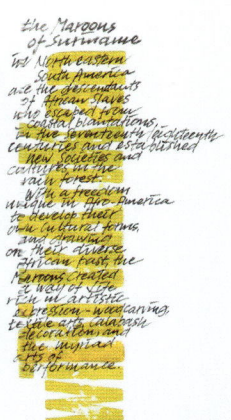

Ron Flu, *Bananenventer* ('Banana hawker'), oil on linen, 100x60 cm, 1982. Acquired 8 August 1984

Another work by Ron Flu was acquired more recently. However, this is a very strong painting by this realist painter, sharply expressing his grim view of society.

Jules Brand-Flu, *Volle maan* ('Full moon'), acrylic on linen, 80x100 cm, date unknown. Acquired 14 June 2006

Jules Brand-Flu is known for his fine stained-glass work. De Surinaamsche Bank has a stained-glass window designed by him, as well as a painting by him inspired by this technique. The work shown here, which currently hangs in the Suritrust building, is different from his usual output, but it certainly shows his craftsmanship. Jules Brand-Flu has been involved in maintaining the DSB collection for years.

René Tosari, *Beeld en toenadering* ('Image and approach'), oil on linen, 96x88 cm, 1990. Acquired in (or around) 1990

René Tosari's work is mainly characterised by a large dose of social engagement combined with a unique style. The combination of acrylic and oil paint is a technique he has mastered like no other.

Cliff San A Jong, *Chinees koppel* **('Chinese couple'), oil on linen, 100x100 cm, date unknown. Acquired 31 May 2011**

Few artists in Suriname have mastered the technique of painting as well as Cliff San A Jong, with his magical-realist style. He is also known for his portraits in this style.

Anand Binda, *Boten na de storm* **('Boats after the storm'), oil on canvas, 50x60 cm, 2005. Acquired 19 March 2008**

Anand Binda's work is Impressionist. With subtle colour play in what at first appears to be coarse strokes, he transmits the beauty and atmosphere of what he depicts in a very pure way.

Carlos Blaaker, *Metafoor* ('Metaphor'), acrylic on linen, 100x100 cm, 2010. Acquired 31 October 2012

During the 1980s, Carlos Blaaker spent a long time studying in the United States. He returned to Suriname for a few years, where he worked in the pop art tradition. Blaaker is currently living on the island of Curacao. The DSB collection features several of his works, in which his evolution is evident, of which this is the most recent acquisition.

Kenneth Flijders, *Beweging* ('Movement'), mixed media on hardboard, 33.5x47.5 cm, 2005. Acquired 17 November 2005

Kenneth Flijders has been working at the Nola Hatterman Art Academy as a teacher for years, and is one of the most important artists from the Readytex Art Gallery. Flijders likes to experiment with materials such as paper made of banana fibres or coconut husks.

George Struikelblok, *untitled*, **mixed media on canvas, 147.5x55cm, 2005. Acquired 6 June 2005**

George Struikelblok is one of the artists who, after his education on Jamaica, developed in an unprecedented manner. His early themes were death and loss, but now it is all about family life and love. He currently has his own studio: Atelier Struikelblok.

Marcel Pinas, *untitled*, **acrylic on canvas, 150x180 cm, date unknown. Acquired 19 August 2013**

Marcel Pinas is mainly known for his impressive installations. His entire oeuvre centres on the preservation of culture, for which Pinas takes his inspiration from his Ndyuka background. His aim is to make his district of birth, Marowijne, Suriname's art district *par excellence*.

Kurt Nahar, *What's left of nature*, mixed media on canvas, 72x76 cm, 2001. Acquired 6 December 2013

Kurt Nahar is known for his gloomy work in which the December killings of 1982 are often the central theme. Nahar is a former student – and now teacher – at the Nola Hatterman Art Academy, and he made the trip to Jamaica as well. Private collectors buy this kind of work less frequently; its inclusion in a corporate collection is therefore all the more important.

Anand Dwarka, *Sardien* ('Sardine'), acrylic on canvas, 90x123 cm, 2005. Acquired 3 March 2006

A piece from Anand Dwarka's early years. Women are a recurring theme in this young artist's work.

Sri Irodikromo, *Kolibri* ('Hummingbird'), acrylic and mixed media on canvas, 70x80 cm, 2012. Acquired 22 January 2013

Sri Irodikromo made a great impression with 'Ingiwinti', her enormous work for the *Paramaribo SPAN* exhibition. This piece may be much smaller, but Sri's characteristic 'handwriting' is clearly evident: with batik prints and symbols in paint, and very colourful.

Dhiradj Ramsamoedj, *This is a Picture of a Mystery*, oil on canvas, 141.5x100 cm, 2010. Acquired 4 November 2010

Dhiradj Ramsamoedj takes his inspiration from his East Indian ancestors and culture. Besides that, he also expresses his somewhat pessimistic view of humanity in his work. His large figures made of iron wire and small pieces of coloured cloth, the so-called flexible men, have made a big impression at several important exhibitions around the world.

Shaundell Horton, *Expectation*, 60x70 cm, 2012. Acquired 22 January 2013

Born in Guyana but raised in Suriname, Shaundell Horton graduated from the Nola Hatterman Art Academy in 2011. Her work, which at times seems somewhat collage-like, contains many references to her Guyanese roots.

EdKe, *Darkened*, mixed media on canvas, 70x70 cm, 2011. Acquired 22 January 2013

EdKe, an alias of Miguel Keerveld, likes to make his audience think. Contradictions, life and death, semblance and reality: the artist philosophises, and his audience can join in.

Piet van Leeuwaarde, *Troon van Babylon* ('Throne of Babylon'), 180 cm wide x 110 cm high x 80 cm deep, wooden sculpture, probably 2005. Acquired 21 December 2005
An artist who was less well-known in Suriname than he deserved to be, Piet van Leeuwaarde was a mystic, *bon vivant*, and gifted sculptor. He mainly worked with sea grape, a kind of wood that is slightly softer than mahogany.

Armand Masé, *Vrouw, lezend* ('Woman, reading'), mahogany sculpture, 25 cm high, 2006. Acquired 15 February 2006
Armand Masé has been working as a sculptor for almost 40 years. His greatest inspiration is the human body. He manages to bring the wood to life.

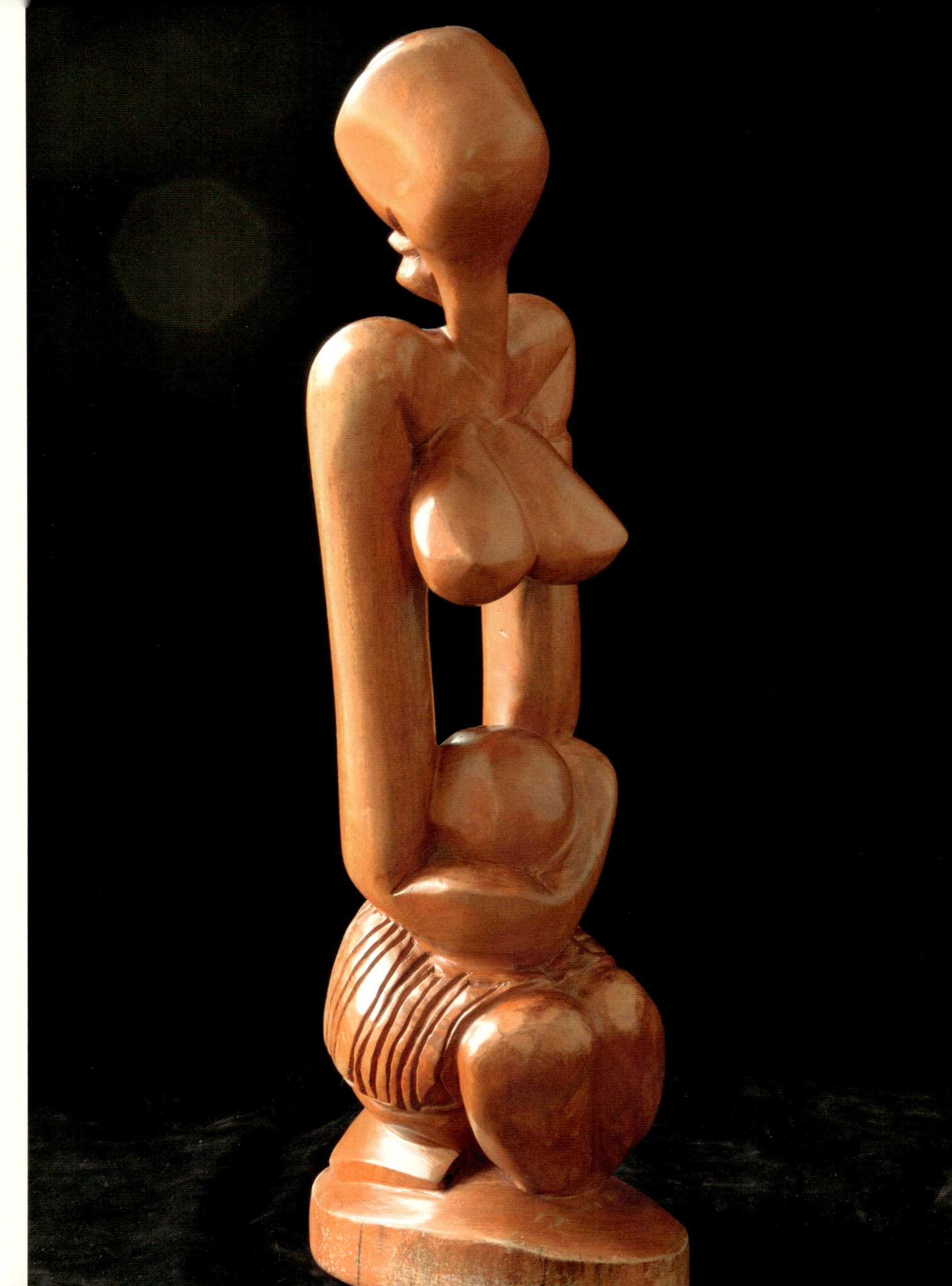

Milton Masé, *Moeder en kind* ('Mother and Child'), mahogany sculpture, 20 cm diameter x 57 cm high, date unknown. Acquired 18 November 2013

DSB acquired several works by Milton Masé in 2013. 'Moeder en kind' stands out because of the clean lines of the mother figure.

Rinaldo Klas, *Revolt chair*, painted chair, year unknown. Acquired 20 March 2008

There always have to be exceptions to the rules: they are not paintings, nor sculptures, and yet they are part of the

Erwin de Vries, *Revolt chair*, painted chair, year unknown. Acquired 20 March 2008

DSB art collection. A good example is these painted 'Revolt chairs' by Rinaldo Klas and Erwin de Vries.

Casper Hoogzaad, *untitled*, tempera on canvas, 150x100 cm, 2010. Acquired 16 March 2010
One of the very few acquisitions of work by a non-Surinamese artist in the DSB collection. Casper Hoogzaad was one of the artists exhibited at *Paramaribo SPAN*. He worked in Suriname before, and at that time started making paint from natural ingredients, using techniques that were centuries old. These pieces were created with authentic Surinamese paint, blended by the artist himself.

Rinaldo Klas, *Goudkoorts I* ('Gold Rush I'), acrylic on canvas, 187x144 cm, 2012. Acquired 19 July 2012
There are other works by Rinaldo Klas in the DSB collection. This painting is from *Gold Rush*, a Klas solo exhibition from 2012. This recent acquisition perfectly fits DSB's policy of supporting nature conservation and a clean environment.

What is striking after this little 'tour' is that the collection contains mostly paintings, and a few not very large sculptures. Almost every important name is represented – besides the artists presented here, this also includes people like Soeki Irodikromo, Ruben Karsters, Hans Lie, John Lie A Fo, Lilian de Vries-Abegg, Armand Baag, Kit-Ling Tjon Pian Gi, Robby Autar, and many others, all of whom were included in *Zichtbaar*. DSB also structurally acquires work by young and upcoming artists. If one remark were to be made regarding a possible gap in the collection, it would be that it features hardly any installations, video art, or other more experimental art forms.

At the front line

When it comes to art, De Surinaamsche Bank has frequently set an example, and on several different fronts. Not only did Jozef Brahim and Rudi de la Fuente lay the foundation for the collection, but also the annual reports from the time they were active were so artistically designed by De la Fuente that they became instant collector's items. After that, both directors Edward Muller and Sigmund Proeve kept the 'flame of art' alive. The flow of new acquisitions never stopped, and the importance of maintaining the collection was never in doubt.

The bank has proven time and time again that it is dedicated and has good insight when it comes to art and culture. Art critic Rob Perrée, a connoisseur of Surinamese visual art, foresees great opportunities for DSB to enlarge the visibility of the collection in the future. 'The bank could organise activities around the collection, such as guided tours for the public on set dates. This would increase the value of the collection too, as the value of a work of art is partly determined by its appeal. Art pieces stored in a bank will be less valuable than more publicly accessible works. Their value will also increase if pieces are reproduced in a publication or a digital medium.'

Perrée sees other possibilities for DSB to maintain its vanguard role in the field of art. 'The bank could do more than simply collecting: for instance, facilitating cheap funding for the acquisition of art, or financially supporting art or artist's projects. The bank has to be aware that it can play an active role in the development of Surinamese art.'

The economic importance of a corporate collection

DSB sees its art acquisitions as an investment. The importance is obvious to the company: not only are the works interesting assets, they also serve as beautiful decorations for the various company buildings, as a contribution to the development of the visual arts sector, and as a way to provide openings to young artists. Nevertheless, most Surinamese companies seldom or never add their collections to their annual reports as an asset. Instead, the acquisition of art is usually entered as an expense in their profit and loss statements. Why? Do entrepreneurs not think about art in this way? Or is the material value of art less than its sentimental worth?

DSB always has room in its offices for art. This painting by Cliff San A Jong is titled *Zwangere vrouw* ('Pregnant woman'); also see p. 154.
Collection DSB

Readytex Art Gallery director Monique NouhChaia SookdewSing believes you can definitely look at art from a commercial viewpoint, and also from an intellectual one. 'It is, in fact, a body of thought you're buying. A collection confirms the value of it.' The gallery owner often sees common ground between entrepreneurship and creativity. 'There's a lot of inspiration to be had from freethinking artists. This is what makes creative people interesting to the community. They document time for us in a different way from historians. Art creates an atmosphere, an incentive. That is why we should inspire our companies to invest in artists.'

She believes that when building a good corporate collection, it is of great importance to begin with a clear-cut policy. 'My advice to companies assembling a collection is this: make sure there is a leitmotiv. A policy makes a collection a closed, interconnected story. This will give a collection historical value.' Making such a policy is not necessarily difficult, she thinks. 'You could say, for instance: I will collect works of art featuring the colour of my company logo. Or: I will only acquire work from artists younger than 40. You can make your leitmotiv very specific. You don't have to include everything in it.' Apart from that, an active form of marketing is vital. 'DSB did this with its collection with the *Zichtbaar* exhibition and catalogue in 2005. Their art collection has been documented for some decades now, and that adds value to it.'

Step-by-step plan for the development of a (corporate) collection

- Formulate the intention to actively collect art. The company must be fully aware of the fact that with a collection, it supports the body of thought of creative people.

- Appoint a curator (or a curatorial team) who develops a vision for the future: what will the collection look like in X number of years?

- Make sure the company's management commits to the idea. Their support is essential.

- Examine your financial capacity: can funds be allocated to start a (corporate) collection?

- Draw up a plan describing the type of art you want to collect and how you intend to acquire it.

- Treat this plan the way you would treat any business plan.

- Actively promote the collection.

Sources

Discussions, correspondence and interviews with Monique NouhChaia SookdewSing, Rob Perrée and Henna Rellum.

Literature

Binnendijk, C. van & Faber, P., *Beeldende kunst in Suriname. De twintigste eeuw/Visual Art in Suriname. The Twentieth Century.* Amsterdam: Royal Tropical Institute, 2000. (Revised edition of *Twintig jaar beeldende kunst in Suriname 1975-1995*)

Binnendijk, C. van & Faber, P. (comp. and eds.), *Sranan, Cultuur in Suriname.* Amsterdam: Royal Tropical Institute, 1992.

Binnendijk, C. van, *Zichtbaar. Uit de kunstcollectie van De Surinaamsche Bank N.V.* Paramaribo: De Surinaamsche Bank N.V., 2005.

Meijer zu Schlochtern, T. & Cozier, Chr. (eds.), *Paramaribo SPAN. Hedendaagse beeldende kunst in Suriname.* Amsterdam: KIT Publishers, 2010.

NouhChaia SookdewSing, M., 'Bruggen tussen kunst en business', in: *EFM Magazine*, vol. 1, no. 1 (July 2012).

NouhChaia SookdewSing, M., 'Good practices voor het kopen van kunst', in: *EFM Magazine*, vol. 1, no. 2 (October 2012).

NouhChaia SookdewSing, M., 'Hoe maken kunstverzamelaars hun kunstcollectie actief?', in: *EFM Magazine*, vol. 2, no. 3 (January 2013).

NouhChaia SookdewSing, M., 'Kunst en cultuur, waardevolle marketingtools voor Suriname', in: *EFM Magazine*, vol. 2, no. 4 (April 2013).

Visser, M., *Talent. Uit de kunstcollectie van de Centrale Bank van Suriname.* Paramaribo: Central Bank of Suriname, 2007.

Marieke Visser studied journalism and language and literature in the Netherlands. She moved back to Suriname 1993 where she and Karin Lachmising founded Tabiki Productions, a creative communications company, in 2000. As a publicist she now writes about art and culture on behalf of her own press agency, Swamp Fish Press.

Connected, transparent and committed
Serving the Surinamese society for 150 years

LM Publishers
Post Box 40455
3504 AE Utrecht
The Netherlands
info@lmpublishers.nl
www.lmpublishers.nl

© 2015 LM Publishers – Utrecht

Project editor Peter Sanches
Image research Chapters 1 - 5 Peter Sanches
Image research Chapter 6 Theo van Elmpt
Image research Chapter 7 Marieke Visser
English translation LGOC, Amsterdam
Design Ad van Helmond, Amsterdam
Lithography and printing High Trade BV, Zwolle

This is the English translation of the original Dutch text, published as *Verbonden, zichtbaar en betrokken. 150 jaar dienstverlening aan de Surinaamse samenleving* (ISBN 978 94 6022 382 2)

Printed in Slovakia

All rights reserved. No part of this publication may be reproduced, stored in a retrieval system, or transmitted in any form, or by any means, electronic or otherwise, without the prior written permission of the publisher

Every effort has been made to identify, contact and obtain permission from possible copyright holders of images used in this publication. In the event of an oversight, please contact the publisher.

ISBN 978 94 6022 385 3